STEPHANIE PARSONS

PLAY ATTENTION!

A Playful Mindset Meets Academic Content

HEINEMANN
Portsmouth, NH

Heinemann
361 Hanover Street
Portsmouth, NH 03801–3912
www.heinemann.com

Offices and agents throughout the world

© 2021 by Stephanie Parsons

All rights reserved. No part of this book may be reproduced in any form or by any electronic or mechanical means, including information storage and retrieval systems, without permission in writing from the publisher, except by a reviewer, who may quote brief passages in a review.

> *Heinemann's authors have devoted their entire careers to developing the unique content in their works, and their written expression is protected by copyright law. We respectfully ask that you do not adapt, reuse, or copy anything on third-party (whether for-profit or not-for-profit) lesson-sharing websites.*
>
> **–Heinemann Publishers**

"Dedicated to Teachers" is a trademark of Greenwood Publishing Group, Inc.

The author and publisher wish to thank those who have generously given permission to reprint borrowed material:

Graphics on pages 45, 73, and 103 from *New York State Next Generation Mathematics Learning Standards.* Copyright © 2017, New York State Education Department. Used with permission. Please note: The New York State P–12 Common Core Learning Standards, adopted in 2011, will be replaced by the Next Generation Learning Standards beginning in the 2021–2022 school year.

Library of Congress Cataloging-in-Publication Data
Names: Parsons, Stephanie, author.
Title: Play attention! : a playful mindset meets academic content / Stephanie Parsons.
Description: Portsmouth, NH : Heinemann Publishing, [2020] | Includes bibliographical references.
Identifiers: LCCN 2020018793 | ISBN 9780325110073
Subjects: LCSH: Play. | Creative ability in children. | Child development.
Classification: LCC LB1137 .P37 2020 | DDC 372.21—dc23
LC record available at https://lccn.loc.gov/2020018793

Editor: Katie Wood Ray
Production Editor: Sonja S. Chapman
Cover and Interior Designer: Monica Ann Crigler
Typesetter: Shawn Girsberger
Manufacturing: Steve Bernier

Printed in the United States of America on acid-free paper
24 23 22 21 20   MPP   1 2 3 4 5
October 2020 Printing

To Maria Nunziata.
Thank you for making PS 130
such a magical place and for
entrusting me with its continued care.
Y gracias también por
su cariño y apoyo.

★ Contents ★

Acknowledgments *x*

CHAPTER ONE **Why Play?** *1*

Play Is a Basic Need *3*
The Benefits of Playful Classroom Experiences *5*
- ★ Self-Regulation
- ★ Intrinsically Motivated Learning
- ★ Cooperation and Collaboration
- ★ Courage and Risk-Taking
- ★ Flexibility and Creativity
- ★ Abstract Reasoning
- ★ Resilience
- ★ Joy

CHAPTER TWO **A Framework for Play in School** *21*

Invite *23*
Play *26*
- ★ Observe
- ★ Provide Lean Input
- ★ Clean Up

Reflect *36*
Create an Environment That Supports a Playful Mindset *39*

CHAPTER THREE **Material Play** *43*

What Is Material Play? *46*
Consider It *47*
- ★ Establish Management
- ★ Explore Potential
- ★ Discover Concepts

Imagine It 50
- ★ Dry-Erase Surfaces
- ★ Bulletin Boards
- ★ Highlighters
- ★ Art and Craft Supplies
- ★ Science Tools and Materials
- ★ Globes and Map Projections
- ★ Fractions

Plan It 63

CHAPTER FOUR Language Play 69

What Is Language Play? 72

Consider It 74
- ★ Extend Vocabulary
- ★ Understand Grammar and Structure
- ★ Make Sense of and Understand Humor

Imagine It 76
- ★ Breaking Words Together
- ★ One Part, Many Words
- ★ Word Endings
- ★ Word Relatives
- ★ Shades of Meaning
- ★ Expert Words
- ★ Word Textures
- ★ Word Instructions
- ★ Puns and Homophones

Plan It 93

CHAPTER FIVE Collaboration Play *99*
- **What Is Collaboration Play?** *103*
- **Consider It** *104*
  - ★ Become a Learning Community
  - ★ Develop the Skills of Collaborative Discourse
  - ★ Take Ownership of Learning
- **Imagine It** *106*
  - ★ Ideal Learning Environment
  - ★ Soft Start
  - ★ Strategic Mini-Unit
  - ★ Circle of Talkingness
  - ★ Learning Plan
- **Plan It** *116*

References *120*

★ Acknowledgments ★

This book would not exist without the support, input, collaboration, and inspiration of so many people.

Christina Kelly and Huck Parsons-Kelly, my family, are an unfailing source of comfort, care, and, most of all, joy. Writing a book while doing my job as a full-time school administrator has taken me away from them more than I'd like to admit. I'm so grateful for Christina's support and encouragement and Huck's patience and willingness to help me find ways to make learning feel playful. I especially treasure their frequent reminders that "if you're writing a book about play, you should come and play with us!"

My very first editor and good friend since adolescence, Kate Montgomery, talked me through early drafts and asked the kind of astute questions I needed to find my focus. Margaret LaRaia, my second editor, helped me find a coherent thread within the shifting haystack/tsunami of ideas I kept bringing her. It has been my abundant good fortune to have Katie Ray as my third editor. She had a vision of what this book could be long before I did and has brought exactly the right combination of guidance, inspiration, encouragement, patience, and impatience that I needed throughout five years (did I mention patience?) and hundreds of pages of hits and misses.

The transformation that turns a bunch of boring-looking typed pages into the gorgeous object you're now holding in your hands is pure magic. The production and design team at Heinemann infused this book with such a spirit of play. The design and marketing teams asked me such thoughtful questions and took time to really listen to my not-brief answers. I deeply appreciate the care they took to include my quirks in their coordinated efforts.

A few friends have been indispensable thought-partners. Donna Santman has always been game to talk me through some unconventional idea, digging in and making it smarter with me. Kathy Collins appreciates the importance of fun and humor in learning more than anyone I know, and her thoughts are like gold. Ginny Lockwood is human glitter, bringing enthusiasm and energy to every conversation about the rich work of teaching. Melissa Singer came into my classroom like a ray of sunshine (forgive the cliché, but in Melissa's case this is exactly the correct phrase). She spent many hours with me, puzzling over materials and invitations and teaching me a lot with her subtle, yet effective teacher moves.

PS 130, The Parkside School, is my second family. I'm eternally grateful to Jenny Humphrey for bringing me into this warm community. Maria Nunziata has taught me more than I ever thought there was to know about having a vision for education and inspiring others to embrace it. She has consistently reminded me to "dream big" as I've worked to incorporate play into meaningful learning. The collected wisdom and experience of Meredith Jose, Carrie Saffady, Dana Dillon, and Cyrena Leung, the rest of our cabinet, has fed my brain and expanded my thinking about play and inquiry. Mauren Campbell generously agreed to read multiple drafts, offering insightful feedback that helped me be as clear and practical as possible.

The vision of playful learning in upper elementary grades would be an empty one without amazing teachers to breathe life into it. Many of the examples in this book were possible only because teachers at PS 130 collaborated with me and with one another to create thoughtful explorations. Their willingness to try new ideas and their generous reflection on the process has brought a lot of joy to a lot of children.

CHAPTER ONE

WHY PLAY?

The very existence of youth is due in part to the necessity for play; the animal does not play because he is young, he has a period of youth because he must play.
—Karl Groos

Imagine this: You're an upper elementary or middle school teacher, and somehow you find yourself walking in the primary hallway or wing of a school.

You stop to peek into a kindergarten classroom during that magical event known as choice time. You know you're supposed to go copy a very important practice sheet for the state test, or maybe you need to grade that giant stack of literary essays. But from inside the classroom a tiny face catches your eye.

"Are you hungry?" the little boy asks. He's working with a few other impossibly small children in a play kitchen area.

"What do you have?" You ask. A girl comes over and hands you a paper labeled, *menu*. There are some pictures of food labeled with a few letters.

"Today we're serving clams and oatmeal."

"Wow! I'll have some of each," you say. She writes your order on a small pad and asks what you'll have to drink. "Hot chocolate? Or orange juice?"

"That's a tough one. They're both so good with clams. I guess I'll go for the hot chocolate, though."

The kids work as a team to get plates and a cup, serve from the pots on the stove, and pour from a teakettle. They bring your order and you eat it with your hands. The boy gives you a cloth napkin, which you use to wipe the imaginary food from your hands and face.

"That was amazing! I'm going to go write a Yelp review of this place right now!" you say.

The kids look at you quizzically as you return the dishes and make your way back to your very important work.

You just played! Sure, it was fun and cute, but you also did something really important for your brain. You adopted a *playful mindset.* You just created space for possibilities you hadn't imagined before. Clams and oatmeal on the same menu, a meal consisting of these paired with hot chocolate. Dining with no utensils, but, somehow, a cloth napkin. Fifteen minutes ago this combination of variables didn't exist in your vision of how things tend to go, but now it does. Congratulations! This microexpansion of your worldview happens every time your vision of what's possible takes in something new. You were willing to

try something in your imagination that you not only wouldn't have tried, but—and this is the crucial piece—was something that wouldn't even have *occurred* to you to try. "Clams and hot chocolate. Of course!"

Playful experiences like these create pathways in the brain that enable us to consider more readily unusual, inventive, creative, resourceful ways of doing the things we need to do. These are also the pathways needed to solve problems that haven't been solved before and to create things that didn't exist before. These benefits combine and work together to feed a mindset that is flexible, creative, and courageous.

Play Is a Basic Need

As humans, we need to play. I don't mean this like, "I need those shoes" but like, "I need oxygen." Most animals, and certainly all mammals, play. It's not a luxury that humans developed when, as a result of the agricultural revolution some twelve thousand years ago, we stopped needing to spend every waking moment finding food. Play is an evolutionary necessity, and humans were doing it long before the concept of leisure existed. In the late nineteenth century, evolutionary biologist Karl Groos studied the play of young animals (1898) and, later, humans (1901). He observed that young animals played in ways that foreshadowed their eventual survival needs as adults; young predators played at stalking and chasing, young prey played at running away and dodging, young primates played at climbing and swinging. Like all mammals, humans play to develop and maintain the skills we need as adults.

Our survival as humans depends on a complex set of skills, and the variety of human play reflects that complexity. We play with language to learn how it works, and doesn't work, as effective communication with our social groups. In play we learn what our bodies can and can't do. Through play we learn how things work in the world around us—how objects feel and fit together and what they do when they're hit, thrown, banged together, or, in the case of that blue marble I recently found in the toilet, eaten. We create pretend worlds and play within them as practice for navigating the "real" world. As children, we played or pretended our way into almost everything we do as adults. And many adults assert that maintaining a sense of play is vital to their best innovative and creative work. Play helps us grow up happy, healthy, and able to face life's challenges.

Although it's clear that play is integral to human development, somewhere along the way educational policy veered away from educational theory, and *play* became a four-letter word. The decline of free, self-directed play has been

as steep outside of school as in school, and I believe we have suffered more than we've gained.

Studies involving animals have shown that a lack of play in youth leads to deficits in social and emotional regulation (Pellis, Pellis, and Himmler 2014; LaFreniere 2011). The same studies, for obvious ethical reasons, can't be done with human subjects. Except, in a way, they already have, and the results are equally alarming. Peter Gray (2011, 2015) writes extensively about the devastating consequences of the decline and marginalization of play in America over the last fifty-odd years. Without play, Dr. Gray cautions, we don't magically identify another source of all these benefits; we just lose them. In articles, blog posts, TED Talks, and his book, *Free to Learn* (Gray 2015), he has sounded the alarm about the *causative* (not merely correlative) link between less play and more psychopathology in young people. For over half a century, free play for American kids has been squeezed into smaller and smaller time frames. It's not a coincidence that over those same fifty-plus years, diagnoses of depression, anxiety, and behavior disorders have increased at the same rate that time spent playing has fallen. Nor is the fact that many employers struggle to find workers with independent initiative and problem-solving skills unrelated to the decrease in play. It's a bitter irony that in providing more structured activities outside of school, longer school days, and more rigorous curricula, we have raised children who are less prepared for a successful adulthood.

The prohibition of play in schools is misguided, but I have good news for teachers who want it back. Purposeful playful experiences can occur within existing curricular and pedagogical mandates. Play adds value to what we are already doing in our classrooms, and even helps us do it better.

The Benefits of Playful Classroom Experiences

Play benefits people, and society as a whole, in a number of ways, many of which can be achieved through playful classroom experiences. When we tell students what is kind and unkind, safe and unsafe, sound and unsound, reasonable and unreasonable, good and bad, they no longer have any opportunity to learn to make judgments for themselves, socially or academically. In contrast, if we create times when we're not telling students what to do and when to do it, we give the gift of self-regulation. If we establish a culture of process over product, we give the gift of courage. If we shift focus away from assignments and grades and toward problem-solving, we give the gifts of flexibility and creativity. If we let collaboration happen organically and voluntarily, we give the gifts of social regulation and democracy. All of these gifts add up to the biggest gift for us and our students—joy.

Viola Spolin (2000), originator of Theater Games and a formative influence in the development of America's first improvisational theater company, Chicago's Second City, puts it this way: "Outside of play there are few places where children can contribute to the world in which they find themselves. Their world, controlled by adults who tell them what to do and when to do it, offers them little opportunity to act or to accept community responsibility." By creating playful conditions, we "offer students the opportunity for equal freedom, respect, and responsibility within the community of the classroom" (3).

Later in this book, I'll describe some individual playful experiences as well as ways to encourage a playful mindset across the day and year. First I want to take a closer look at the ways play benefits students, as learners and as humans.

All of these benefits are interrelated, overlapping with one another. Being more intrinsically motivated leads to more risk-taking, which leads to increased flexibility, for example, but considering them separately helps us understand what it is about play that makes it so transformational to students' growth.

Self-Regulation

Management is not the most exciting facet of our work as teachers, but without it, well, the classroom can feel like a pretty insecure place for everyone. The skills of self-regulation—impulse control, emotional intelligence, the capacity to act according to social norms (and class rules)—are not skills I used to associate with letting kids play in my classroom. I was so misguided! Vygotsky (1978) figured it out before my mother was even born; play is how children acquire these very competencies.

In their dramatic play, young children often cast themselves as people in familiar situations—parents, doctors, teachers, salespeople, and so on. When playing together in a pretend scenario, children follow the rules that apply to it. A group of kindergartners playing restaurant have an unspoken agreement to do things like sit at a table and look at a menu, take orders and bring food to the table, cook the food, and wash the dishes. Moreover, the diners might even order something they would never eat at home and happily gobble it down in the "restaurant." A player in this scenario is not going to suddenly lie down under the table to find the cause of engine trouble. Vygotsky (1978) called dramatic play a child's way of creating her own zone of proximal development for living:

> This strict subordination to rules is quite impossible in life, but in play it does become possible: thus, play creates a zone of proximal development of the child. In play a child always behaves beyond his average age, above his daily behavior; in play it is as though he were a head taller than himself. (102)

In this way, children practice taking actions that are guided by thought and reason, rather than by impulse.

As children get older, they continue to develop the self-regulation competencies that began in their early play. Self-directed play among groups of children is still guided by rules that the players agree to and requires children to navigate social relationships in increasingly deft ways. Peter Gray (2015) explores this idea in an extended comparison between an informal neighborhood game of stickball and a Little League baseball game. In the stickball game, the players agree on the rules and can modify them if necessary to keep the game going and make sure everyone is having fun. When conflicts arise, the players argue, negotiate, or compromise so they can get back to playing. In the informal game, teamwork is about working together in the moment; players may change teams if circumstances demand it, and the teams may form differently on a different day. All of these qualities of the informal game support an attitude that really does value playing well and having fun over winning.

In a formal Little League game, adults and external forces render players unable to practice these self-regulation skills. In Little League, the rules are the rules. They don't change if someone is just beginning to learn the game or the field is muddy. When conflicts arise, the adults take over. Teams are set, separated, and defined as much by their uniforms as by the rivalries that arise among them. And, of course, the goal is to win. Organized sports can be great for some kids, but they're not a replacement for self-directed play (Gray 2015, 157–63). When adults make the rules and call it "play," we've robbed children of an important developmental need, which is to be in a situation and have to navigate it, figuring out for oneself what makes sense. *This* is how children learn to self-regulate, not by having their behavior always mediated by adult input.

Through playful exploration in the classroom, we can create conditions under which children practice self-regulation. As you'll read about later in this book, one simple and concrete way I have capitalized on this is to invite students to play with fun materials that I eventually hope to use in a more limited academic context. Rather than telling students what they can and can't do, I introduce the materials and ask them what makes sense. As they play, engaging with one another and the materials, children bump up against situations that stimulate their sense of order, fairness, care, and fun. They end up making reasonable rules and adhering to them more faithfully than they would to externally imposed rules.

Intrinsically Motivated Learning

Because an essential feature of play is the perception of choice, play, by definition, is guided by intrinsic interests and motivations. In the 1970s, Richard Ryan and Edward L. Deci, clinical and social scientists, began to develop a theory of human motivation and personality that focused on intrinsic motivation. Since then, social scientists and researchers around the world have taken on the question of how intrinsic versus extrinsic motivation affects the outcomes of human endeavors. The research that has contributed to self-determination theory has shown, in many contexts, that intrinsic motivation leads to enhanced learning, performance, creativity, and social-emotional wellness. By giving students meaningful choice, we build intrinsic motivation into their activities, fostering their natural tendencies to be curious, to seek out challenges, and to develop skills, knowledge, and understanding (Ryan and Deci 2000).

The degree of playfulness children feel in an activity is directly related to the amount of choice they believe themselves to have (King and Howard 2016); the more control over choice we can hand over to students, the more playful (and intrinsically motivated) their actions will be. This applies certainly to experiences labeled explicitly as play, such as when I put Array Play or Fantasy Play on the schedule. A subtler, yet equally powerful stimulus for intrinsic motivation comes from a sense of playfulness that runs through the day and infuses the classroom environment. Students who have choice in how to engage with

the curriculum are more intrinsically motivated to do so, taking more ownership of the learning process. What to read and write, which angle of a historical time period to study, how to approach a math or science question, and how to present one's work are some of the choices we can offer to increase engagement.

Of course, the amount of choice we can give our students is limited by several factors related to time, space, materials, and regulations. It's not an all-or-nothing proposition, though! There are many shades of gray—shades of *play*—between total freedom and total control. If we see this vast middle ground as a continuum of choice, teachers can extend many of the benefits of play to students in classrooms by considering the amount and kind of choice we give to children.

How we give choice also matters. Students must perceive that they have meaningful choice, but this is not as easy as it sounds. Actually, it may not even sound that easy. I can hear myself saying, "Are you sure you really want to try *that*?" The second we take away choice, though, or even imply that there are good and bad choices, an activity stops being

playful and we may lose the intrinsic motivation and, hence, the learning benefits. So we have to be careful! If we're going to offer choice, we have to accept all (safe) choices. My students have tested me, positive that there was a catch—that I couldn't possibly really mean to let them make the choices I was offering. When I feel myself wanting to limit the amount of choice, I try to remember to be open to amazement, trusting that students will discover something that benefits the whole learning community. I also remind myself that children who perceive their play to be limited by adult rules and instructions show poorer problem-solving skills, less motivation, and lower engagement than other children *performing the same tasks* (McInnes [2009], as cited in King and Howard [2016]).

Cooperation and Collaboration

Viola Spolin (2000) argues that the democratic nature of play supports children in making decisions that benefit a shared purpose:

> Many of the skills learned in playing are social skills. Most games worth playing are highly social and have a problem that needs solving within them—an objective point in which each individual must become involved with others while attempting to reach a goal. (3)

My own observations and personal classroom experience have revealed that the more an activity feels like play, the more cooperative and collaborative it is. We've all seen collaborative learning activities go remarkably well or horribly wrong. When they go well, students work together and get along as equals. They jump into the work, engaging together in authentic and spirited communication. They may argue or negotiate, but their shared purpose helps them find compromise. Their talk seems freer and more filled with the spirit of "What if?" as they plan together how to go about doing what they need to do. They cooperate in dividing the work, enthusiastically supporting one another to benefit the group. When children do normal human things that can get in the way of collaboration—boss other group members around, try to get out of doing something undesirable, feel lost and not know how to ask for help, become competitive, to name a few—the group is able to right itself. And in the end, they have *fun*! When it doesn't go well, it seems like the teacher has to become the project manager and group therapist for everyone. It's exhausting, totally the opposite of fun, and we all end up wondering if the intended learning actually happened.

Humans have been developing culture through play since there were humans. We've known that playfulness is good for society (group peace and harmony, efficacy, etc.) for a long time. In his analysis of research on hunter-gatherer groups, Peter Gray (2009) notes that humor and playfulness, in both adults and children, informed their systems of governing, religion, productive work, and education:

> Play and humor lay at the core of hunter-gatherer social structures and mores. Play and humor were not just means of adding fun to their lives. They were means of maintaining the band's existence—means of promoting actively the egalitarian attitude, extensive sharing, and relative peacefulness for which hunter-gatherers are justly famous and upon which they depended for survival. (476–477)

By injecting a spirit of play into the classroom, we expose students to situations that make them internalize the collaborative qualities that they will depend on as adults.

Even in experiences where children are working or playing independently, there is still a collaborative atmosphere, as everyone contributes to the playfulness that infuses the classroom. Eliminating competition helps students wish well for one another. Also, even when playing alone, the choice to collaborate is a powerful one, based on the intrinsic purpose of all the players.

Courage and Risk-Taking

In recent years, many community organizations, independent schools, and camps have put forth the idea that allowing more risk in children's play leads to increased health, self-esteem, judgment, and pleasure. Children develop "risk competence" by trying things that most adults forbid nowadays because they are dangerous ("You'll put an eye out!"). Advocates for more risky play argue that by taking all of the danger out of children's play in the name of protection from injury, we've actually exposed them to more harm (Gray 2015; Almon 2013; Eichsteller and Holthoff 2009). Children learn to assess risk and make decisions about whether or how to, for example, climb a tree, cut a piece of wood, or make a fire, by doing these things—not by being told *not* to do them or by being hovered over the whole time and micromanaged. In fact, forbidding or micromanaging potentially dangerous tasks hinders children's ability to learn to make safe and sound judgments for themselves.

The need for children to learn how to take risks through play is a biological one. Extensive study of play in animals reveals much about the importance of play for humans. Play during youth induces structural changes within the brain, resulting in improved executive functioning and social competency. A key feature of youthful play is that it provides an experience of unpredictability and loss of control that, unlike outside of play, is rewarding and pleasurable (Pellis, Pellis, and Himmler 2014). Facing uncertainty in play helps animals (including us) deal appropriately and effectively with "the unexpected vicissitudes of life." Play teaches us how to take risks and face uncertainty, because life requires it.

The benefits of becoming more confident and competent risk-takers also applies to academic and social learning. We don't learn anything new by staying close to what we already know and understand, nor can we learn in situations that spark fear and anxiety. Senninger's Learning Zone Model ([2000], as cited in Watling [2016] and Eichsteller and Holthoff [2009]) suggests that learning happens when we venture outside of the Comfort Zone, but not so far that we enter the Panic Zone. In the Learning Zone, we face some discomfort and challenge in exploring the unknown, but we do so with a growth mindset. The very

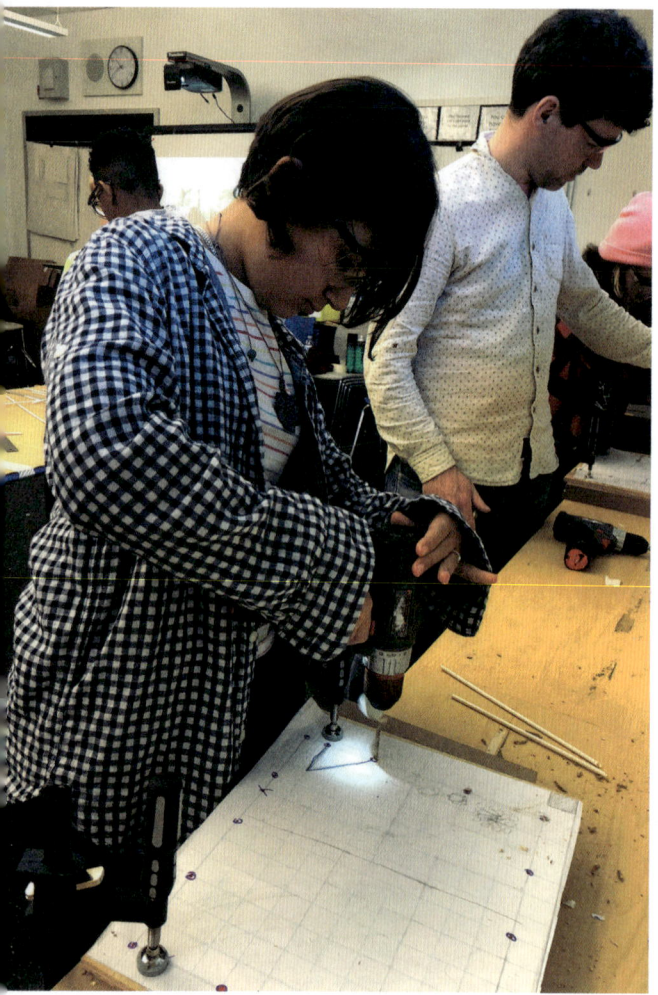

existence of the Learning Zone depends on what Carol Dweck (2016) calls "the power of *yet*," which helps us persevere through difficulty and failure; *I can't do this* yet, *but I will if I keep trying*.

When students don't seem to have a growth mindset for learning academic content, it's as if the Learning Zone has shrunk to nothing, leaving no distance between feeling comfortable and panicking. These students often fear open-ended exploration but thrive in an environment where success depends on getting a certain outcome or answer. On assessments and evaluations, the risk of not being able to perform according to seemingly arbitrary externally imposed criteria leads straight to panic. For students approaching or in adolescence, this is especially true. The added pressure of maintaining an outward appearance makes any kind of failure mortifying. Because playful experiences offer so many points of entry, they facilitate a gradual opening up of students who avoid risk.

Flexibility and Creativity

My brother, Fletcher, is a civil engineer. In his work he hires and oversees people working on a range of projects. He recently complained to me that for the past several years it had been difficult to find people who were actually ready to work on these projects, despite college or graduate educations. He told me of a new hire who had strong technical skills but was unable to make decisions about what to do when. Several times a day she would come to him with questions and problems, needing his approval and direction to continue. She needed to be brave enough to make an independent decision instead of waiting for an assignment. She needed to be flexible enough to face unexpected challenges. She needed to be creative enough to use her skills in new ways. In short, she needed a playful mindset.

Tony Wagner makes the case for rethinking education more fully and persuasively in his book, *Creating Innovators: The Making of Young People Who Will Change the World* (Wagner and Compton 2015). Traditional educational models prepare students to regurgitate and comply, whereas our world is increasingly demanding people who are able to think outside of limits, rather than staying within them. He says, "Increasingly in the twenty-first century, what you know is far less important than what you can do with what you know. The interest in and ability to create new knowledge to solve new problems is the single most important skill that all students must master today" (142).

Multiple studies have demonstrated that play increases creativity. In Kathy Sylva's classic study ([1977] as cited in Garvey [1990]), children were given two sticks and a clamp and asked to use them to reach a piece of chalk that was out of reach. Some children were allowed to play freely with the sticks and clamp before the task, some were taught explicitly how to clamp the sticks together, and some didn't see the materials at all before the task. The groups who played and were taught explicitly both performed the task correctly more than the control group. The group who played, however, exhibited more persistence and motivation than the group who was shown how to connect the sticks.

Entering a process with a playful mindset means seeing what didn't work as a new challenge and not a failure. Embracing these challenges opens the door for creative problem-solving—thinking "out of the box." The ability or ease of taking risks allows the mind to wander further away from the boundaries of what's known—the comfort zone. Armed with the question of "What if?" and unencumbered by the notion that it has to work a certain way, the aim shifts from correctness to discovery.

Abstract Reasoning

We used to think of the developmental shift from concrete to abstract thought as a linear progression, similar to physical growth; once you reach four feet, you don't go back to three feet eleven inches. Surprise! It's a lot more complicated and

nuanced than that. We now know that our capacity for abstract thought is related to experiences we've had and our state of mind. As we gain more experiences, we are increasingly able to use imagination to make things that were once abstract become concrete.

Consider the equation $2 + 2 = 4$. For most kindergartners, this is a very abstract concept. These symbols are just squiggles. The act of counting out two pebbles from a pile of pebbles and sliding them away, then counting out two more pebbles and sliding them over to the first two, and then counting the four separated pebbles, is much more concrete. As adults, our years of life have given us the experience required to *imagine* situations that would give concrete meaning to $2 + 2 = 4$.

Experiences give us more material to draw on when we're trying to make sense of something unknown or unfamiliar. However, imagination is also required to make the cognitive jump from a known thing to an abstract thing (Gray 2008; Bergen 2009). Barricade, a flame retardant gel used to protect homes and other structures from fires, is a perfect illustration. John Bartlett, founder of Barricade International, was not the first firefighter to notice that used diapers at charred scenes were slimy and gooey, and—critically—unburnt. His imaginative mind *was* the only one to make the leap from this concrete experience to the abstract idea of spraying the soaked diaper gel over a whole house and creating a flameproof barrier. Years of lab experiments later, hundreds of homes have been saved by the stuff (Lewis 2000). If imagination is a muscle, play is the exercise that makes it stronger and more flexible. I might argue that all the people we see as innovative geniuses are not any different from the rest of us except in one regard: they're more playful.

The "accidental" learning that happens in play comes from a willingness to entertain, even embrace, scenarios one's rational mind has never seen before. In school, children may not imagine such a scenario merely because it's not part of the assignment. My own son has frequently sighed with annoyance at my efforts to engage with his learning: "I just have to do what's on the rubric." Playful exploration gives students room to make the discoveries they're ready and motivated to make, independent of the required lessons or your planned teaching. They may solidify concepts they learned about in the past and had not fully attained, or they may begin to develop new conceptual understandings of things beyond the scope of the curriculum.

A more long-term return on an investment in play lies in its role in how humans create culture. In play we explore ideas and emotions beyond our quotidian experiences. In a rational world, where so much depends on what

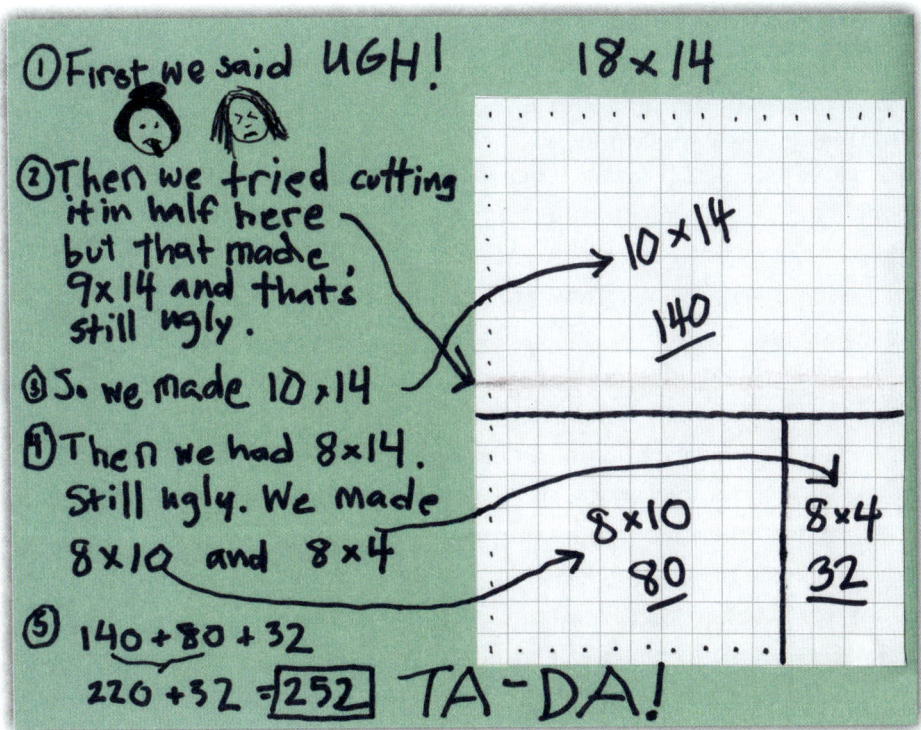

is known and understood, play is the way we safely and fearlessly wrap our minds around the unknown and overwhelming. Why am I me? Why are we here? What happens when we die? A defining feature of human existence is the mind's back-and-forth between rational, pragmatic, concrete living and the search for purpose and meaning that defies rational explanation. Thomas Henricks (2016) argues that play "centers on a tension between different ways of relating to the world" (309). As we have seen, the rules of play are agreed upon and self-imposed by the players. Juxtaposing the rationality that comes from the rules of play with its exuberance, irreverence, and impulsivity, we "explore the widest implications of personal and public existence" (321). This tension between rationality and imagination, by the way, is the very definition of the Learning Zone. We're close enough to the known to feel safe as we imagine what may lie in the vast unknown. Although we're concerned about what our students are learning now, with us, we're also preparing this generation for the time when they are the ones setting the course for the future. Play is how we help them develop a good compass.

Resilience

Brian Sutton-Smith is said to have told a group of fellow play researchers, "We study play because life is crap. Life is crap, and it's full of pain and suffering, and the only thing that makes it worth living—the only thing that makes it possible to get up in the morning and go on living—is play" (De Koven 2016). After chuckling at the tongue-in-cheek manner with which Sutton-Smith described his very serious study, I found myself coming back to this quote. My first connection was personal; I have obsessively sought out humor and playfulness as an antidote to a darkness that has been part of my identity for as long as I remember and which I attribute to years of early childhood trauma. I am certain that my playful mindset has tempered the frightening gravity that trauma survivors know so well and enabled me to have an identity that included something other than "trauma survivor."

Perhaps the reason I've decided to keep this quote here despite my attention to word count is that I'm reminded of play in the face of pain and suffering in more dramatic contexts. During a deadly and destructive war that has been the backdrop of their entire lives, Syrian children play. In fact, children's play during times of war has inspired much academic study by adults who must (reasonably) wonder, "How can fun be had in a time like this?" In his book, *Children and Play in the Holocaust*, George Eisen ([1990], as cited in Gray [2008]) describes in detail the ways that children interred in Nazi ghettos and concentration camps played. As Peter Gray (2008) explains, "They played not because they were oblivious to the horrors around them. Nor did they play as a means to deny those horrors or divert their attention from them. Rather, they played in ways that helped them to understand, confront, and, to the degree possible, deal effectively with those horrors." In every school I've visited or worked with, I've heard stories of children facing some sort of trauma, but it's because of the difficulties faced by *every* child entering or in adolescence that I argue for more play.

Growing up is hard. The brain and body undergo dramatic changes. The powerful need to belong and the equally powerful need to forge an individual identity pull *hard* in opposite directions. David Elkind (1967, 1985) termed two key features of this period of development "imaginary audience" and "personal fable." Briefly, tweens and teens perceive their words and actions to be not only seen but actively watched and evaluated by those around them. The idea of having a constant audience requires one to engage in a constant performance, creating the character one thinks one should be. One trip on a New York City subway at 3:00 p.m. on a weekday will show you exactly what I mean. At the same time, children are ensconced in *personal fable*, the idea that "nothing that is happening to me has ever happened to anyone before and is of epic proportions and will have lasting meaning for the rest of my life, and nobody else is even capable of understanding it, especially adults." My cringe-worthy journals from middle and high school back this up. Navigating these conditions is part of the necessary transition from childhood to adulthood and, like every new thing that we take on, is a bit clumsy in the beginning. The tension is between self-expression and identity on the one hand and life's uncertainty and ambiguity on the other.

Confusion about identity is a normal part of being this age, and rather than be diminished by it, children can be supported within it. They need to be able to try on words and behaviors that push the envelope or explore the boundaries of what is OK and what is not and to do so in a safe space. Playing one's way into different identities is a way of understanding oneself and one's capacity to be who they want to be (rather than some predetermined or externally imposed identity).

Joy

And, of course, in play, we experience joy. After several years in school, many older children seem to believe that play is the opposite of work and that what happens in school is supposed to be work. Brian Sutton-Smith (2001) says that the opposite of play is not work; it's depression. The point of play is not the outcome, but the play itself. In work—indeed, in most of life—we are not ensured of our prospects, so our commitment is tempered by the real possibilities and consequences of failure. In play, without these stakes, we're able to follow our

instincts with "exultant commitment," knowing that whatever happens will be the correct outcome, in contrast to feeling the pressure to arrive at a predetermined outcome. The destinations we *do* arrive at in play lead to "adaptive potentiation," meaning that we gain skills and understandings in play that we then use in our nonplay lives (Sutton-Smith 2001).

Joy is an important *outcome* of play and not just a by-product. The effects of joy on the body, such as dopamine and serotonin release and increased circulation, lead to improved physical and emotional health. Frequent episodes of joy lead to a greater overall sense of well-being or happiness. As a natural antianxiety treatment, joy removes barriers to learning. Experiencing joy with others creates bonds that can withstand the social challenges of being a tween. I think we can all agree that more joy in school is a good thing. In the rest of this book, I hope both to give you some practical, doable ways to play in your classroom and to empower you to invent more.

CHARACTERISTICS OF PLAY

PLAY IS:	
Pleasurable	I know—duh. Play is fun, joyful, and exciting and sometimes involves a sense of humor. Play might also include frustrations, challenges, and fears. Our ability to face these and work through them brings pleasure.
Voluntary	An activity feels more like play if the players perceive that they have choices—whether to play, how the play might go, what to play with, and so on. Perhaps most important is that a player has the choice to quit playing or not to play in the first place.
Active	Playing is *doing*. Whether it's physical or mental, alone or collaborative, with ideas or with tangible things, playing is an active, yet relaxed state. People at play are alert, engaged, and, crucially, unstressed.
Adventurous and Risky	Taking risks is a key component of a growth mindset, as is trying again when something doesn't work out. Play provides a safety net for students to explore the unknown or try new things.
Process Oriented	People at play are concerned primarily with the process of their play, rather than with a preconceived outcome. Motivated from within by their own desire to explore or make things, children shape their explorations as they go (Shipley 2013).
Symbolic and Meaningful	When children imagine and pretend, it's as if they're casting themselves in roles they've never experienced and exploring what those roles might be like. Play helps children visualize abstract concepts, such as fractions or a time when there was no electricity. Perhaps most importantly, imaginary play is children's way to safely explore their current and possible future identities.

A FRAMEWORK FOR PLAY IN SCHOOL

Children learn as they play.
Most importantly, in play children learn how to learn.
—O. Fred Donaldson, Contemporary American martial arts master

When I first started to explore play in my classroom, I was worried about creating a vacuum of order and authority. I had visions of the food fight scene in *Animal House*. It turned out to be a little more like Stockholm syndrome; my students couldn't believe I actually meant to let them play. Their few years of formal schooling had already conditioned them to believe that play is not something that happens in classrooms. For example, listen in to this conversation I had with my fourth-grade class before inviting them to play with plastic polygons from our math manipulatives container.

Maya seemed to speak for the class when she said, "Well, wait a minute, are you talking about school play or just play?"

"Are they different? I mean, usually we just say 'play' whether it's in here or out at recess."

"Yeah, but there's school play and . . . play play," explained Tobias.

"Oh, I see. So, what would you say play play is, and is it really that different from school play?"

Mark added, "Well, in leisure play you don't learn anything but in school play you do."

"If we're really playing, then we can do anything. Like throw things around and stuff. But we can't throw stuff around the classroom," Maya suggested, "That's not what you mean when we're playing in here."

"No, I guess that's true. Do you always throw stuff around when you play play?" I asked.

"We do when we're playing basketball or monkey in the middle, or stuff like that," Eric answered.

"You don't throw things in tag," Daniela mused.

"We don't throw, but we *are* running all over the place, and we can't do that in here either," answered Kian.

"Do throwing and running make it play play and not school play, then?" I asked

"Well, no, not always. I mean, you *can* play without running or throwing . . ." Rowan trailed off. She seemed to be grappling with the question of what makes an activity count as play.

"It seems like throwing things is part of some play, but not all play. I never see you throw stuff when you're playing Scrabble or doing those battles with your fingers, for example."

"Well, no, that wouldn't make sense," Nina explained, "You don't just play with things randomly. A ball is good for throwing and catching, but . . . Hula-Hoops aren't, or cards. You have to play with those differently. It's like the thing you're playing with helps you know how to play."

"Ah, so if I give you these to play with," I said, holding up some of the plastic polygons, "what kind of play makes sense in this classroom with these materials?"

Sammy said, "Not throwing, probably, because there are some really pointy parts."

"Agreed. What else do you see yourself doing with them as soon as you get some into your hands?" I asked.

I listened in as they turned to talk with partners for a half a minute. I heard students talking about making designs, building structures, and layering and

tracing, and that's where most students started. Soon, without prompting from the teachers (we were playing a bit, too!), they were making discoveries about equivalence, angle measure, fractions, and more.

As this conversation reveals, many people have a very narrow definition of play, seemingly characterized by random chaos, but the playful experiences we plan for students to have in school aren't like that at all. Throughout the school day, *predictable* structures help teachers plan and students learn, and planning for play is no different. When students know how an experience tends to go, they can spend their energy engaged in the exploration rather than on learning new routines or protocols every time. The play experiences in this book, varied as they are in purpose, pacing, concept, and materials, follow a predictable cycle of *invite*, *play*, and *reflect*. The elements of the cycle will look a little different across play experiences, but what matters most is that they are consistent. After all, a predictable structure allows wonderfully unpredictable things to happen.

Invite

Every play experience begins with an invitation.

> *I was thinking a way for us to make sense of what we're learning as we read and learn about the genre of fantasy is to create our own fantasy worlds, with their own rules and customs and citizens and types of magic. . . . I have all these different images of fantasy characters and settings, and stuff for you to create others if you need to. Today after you meet with your book clubs, I've planned some extra time for you to discuss whether you want to cocreate a fantasy world and what you need for it.*

A successful invitation functions as a hook—a stimulus of some sort. Much of the literature about play in school, stemming from the work of Reggio Emilia, refers to this part of the process as *provocation*. In considering the developmental qualities of older students, I prefer to think of it as an *invitation*. Yes, we want to provoke students, in the sense of providing the needed stimulus to explore playfully. We also want to honor the older child's powerful need for self-determination and choice, and so we invite them to indulge in their curiosity. I want to be clear that it doesn't actually matter what we call it, though. It matters how we do it. An effective invitation provides points of

In many invitations, the draw of unfamiliar and fun materials creates interest in content learning.

entry for students to playfully explore and manipulate materials and concepts and motivation to express their questions and ideas in a variety of ways.

With an invitation, you need to entice the full range of students, encouraging them to engage in the exploration in different ways, guided by their own curious impulses. You also have to mind the fine line between letting students know you have a purpose in mind and communicating to them that there is, in fact, a "correct" outcome, especially when you're using this activity to support learning about concepts that some students find difficult. The key is to invite them to have a self-directed experience that is driven by their desire to discover, rather than pressure to arrive at an outcome. Consider the difference between "We're doing this to help us learn about fractional equivalence" and "I think we could find out a lot about fractions, and maybe other things, too. I'm always surprised by the different discoveries people make."

You want students to approach their play with a sense of purpose and possibility, and it's helpful to explain the purpose in a way that communicates a desire—a need, even—for students to collaborate. You might simply show and discuss the materials children will be playing with, or you might engage them in conversation about a video, image, text, question, or a combination of these.

After playing with small cubes and grid paper, fourth graders plan how they'll find all possible arrays for eighteen.

When crafting an invitation, consider both the learning you want to support and how you will inspire students' imaginations. You might briefly demonstrate exploring in your own playful way, thinking aloud about the possibilities. Invite students to share their thoughts and questions about how they want the play experience to go.

Once students have experienced lots of play explorations, the invitation becomes routine and you merely have to present an interesting question or some new materials. Children will *know* that they can explore and experiment, and they'll have an expectation of learning or discovering new things, not because you said so, but because they always do. Depending on the nature of the play experience, the invitation might also include one or both of the following:

★ If you need to set up parameters to ensure safety and respect as students play, ask them how it makes sense to have fun and be creative, while making sure nobody gets hurt in any way—physically or emotionally.

★ If your students have had a similar play experience, they may also have ideas about how they want to engage in the process.

Play

Now that you've piqued their interest and curiosity, allow students time to acquaint themselves with the subject of their play (materials, concepts, one another, and so on). Some students will happily jump right in and begin exploring and experimenting, busily manipulating materials and discussing ideas. Others may be hesitant, perhaps believing that an outcome is, in fact, expected and not sure what it is. Some will focus on their exploration with quiet intensity while others excitedly narrate their every move. A quick scan of the classroom will tell you who needs some support in getting started. Once they're underway, you're ready to observe and provide input—questions, thoughts, ideas, suggestions, musings—to support them.

If you are like me, you might find it hard to let go of the reins and just let your students play. Try to enjoy your students' joy. I promise you'll be glad you did! Although you do have to have your teacher eye on the whole class, it can be beneficial for you to play a little, too, and for students to see you as a model of curiosity. Of course, you could play with materials all the time when kids are not in school, but I'm guessing that's not how you usually spend your time.

Observe

Play is a powerful opportunity for assessment, which can inform your instruction in many ways. If you're alert and attentive, you'll learn so much about children individually, not just what they know and don't know but also their personalities, their socio-emotional strengths and needs—who they *are*. As students play, you'll be looking at what they do or make, watching how they use, arrange, or manipulate the materials, and listening to their conversations. You're looking especially for things you can use later when teaching the content formally, as well as possible extensions or assessment ideas. There's a lot of good intel to be mined from students' explorations, and in the chapters that follow, I'll share some questions to guide your observations of different kinds of play.

I also photograph and jot down a lot of what I observe so I can review the information later; lots of things reveal themselves to be interesting or important after the experience is over. Photos are a particularly useful form of documentation that can be revisited later if students erased, wiped away, or dismantled something without documenting it themselves. Voice recording apps are a great way to document role-plays and discussions.

A Framework for Play in School

Manipulating materials adds visual and tactile components to this student's emerging understanding of factors and multiples.

Provide Lean Input

When students are playing, the purpose of your input is either to better understand or to support their intentions without imposing your own. Avoid looking for specific results; instead, guide students toward their own ideal learning outcomes. There's a danger of turning this into another teacher-directed "skewl" activity. Having experimented with the material, concept, or content yourself, or already having a deep familiarity with it, will help you generate questions or suggestions that actually guide and support students' discovery, without leading them away from their self-directed paths. Also, knowing your students well outside of these explorations, combined with thoughtful observation within them, should inform the kind of input that will benefit students most.

Over the years, I've found a few ways to be supportive without being controlling. Some of these are specific to one or two kinds of play while others can work anytime.

Facilitate Student Discovery Versus Imposing an Agenda

You may find yourself having to bite your tongue and sit on your hands to avoid meddling in students' play, especially when it's very exploratory. Sometimes it's because you want to play, too, which you should go ahead and do on your own; it will give you a window into what students are doing. Worse is when you're trying to guide a student toward some discovery or realization that you want them to have. A fine line divides facilitating a student's own direction and steering them in a direction *you're* interested in.

> **Laila is getting ready to write a Hero Story. She has drawn and cut out some of the characters and is starting to act out some possible scenes. I'm tempted to encourage her to start writing the dialogue she's imagining for the scene. Instead, I approach her with curiosity, and she surprises me with a sophisticated discovery about how a writer can reveal character.**
>
> **Me:** What are you finding out?
>
> **Laila:** They have different ways of speaking!
>
> **Me:** What do you mean?
>
> **Laila:** When I was making them talk to each other, the main girl talks kind of slowly and . . . like she's trying to find the right words as she goes. But this woman is different. I know she's bad, but she wants the girl to trust her, so she doesn't talk like a bad person. She's being *too* nice.

Give a Little Nudge Toward Something Big

When you see students that are *so* close to a major conceptual leap, a careful "What if?" can be the catalyst for making that leap. If students are not ready yet, that What if? will fall flat with no harm done and you will have an assessment that tells you what to teach soon. If they are ready, they'll run with it.

Two fifth graders are playing with arrays as a way to approach two-by-two-digit multiplication problems. They have found that a problem can be made easier by breaking up the array into known problems.

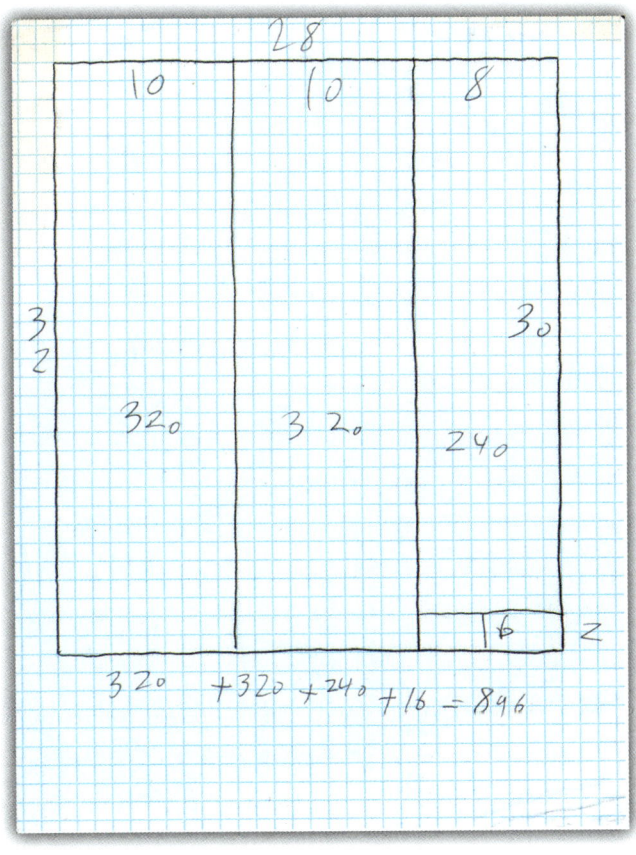

Students' array of 32 by 48 broken into manageable parts

Jordan: We don't know 32 × 28, so we made it 32 × 10, 32 × 10, and then we had 32 × 8. But that was still hard, so we made the last part 30 × 8 and 2 × 8. Now we just add up the whole thing—896!

I wonder if they could visualize this as an unmarked array, which would open all kinds of doors for future problem-solving in multiplication and division.

Play Attention!

Me: Now that you have found this strategy, do you think you could do the same thing if you didn't have grid paper?

Tania: That is way too many squares to draw!

Me: I totally agree! I wonder if there's a way to imagine the squares that *would* be there if you had grid paper. For instance, we have drawn smaller arrays like this. [*I draw a simple* 3 × 4 *unmarked array.*] We don't need to see the squares to know there are twelve of them. We also know that 3 × 4 is equal to (3 × 2) + (3 × 2).

Try it! See what happens!

My model of an unmarked array of 3 by 4

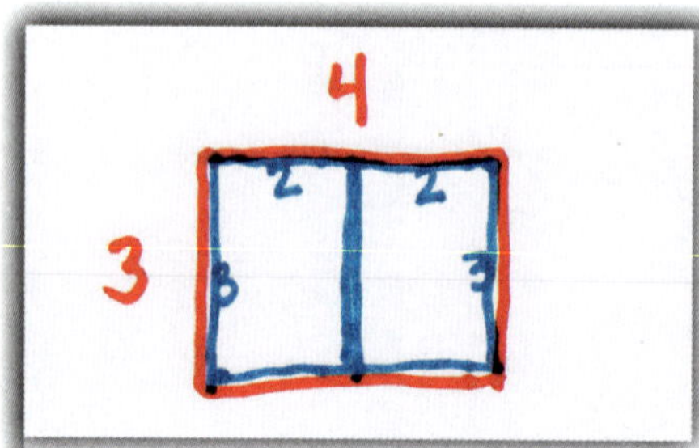

In less space than their original array on grid paper, these students can now use unmarked arrays as a tool for solving larger problems. They even tried splitting the array in a different way and explained why they prefer first way.

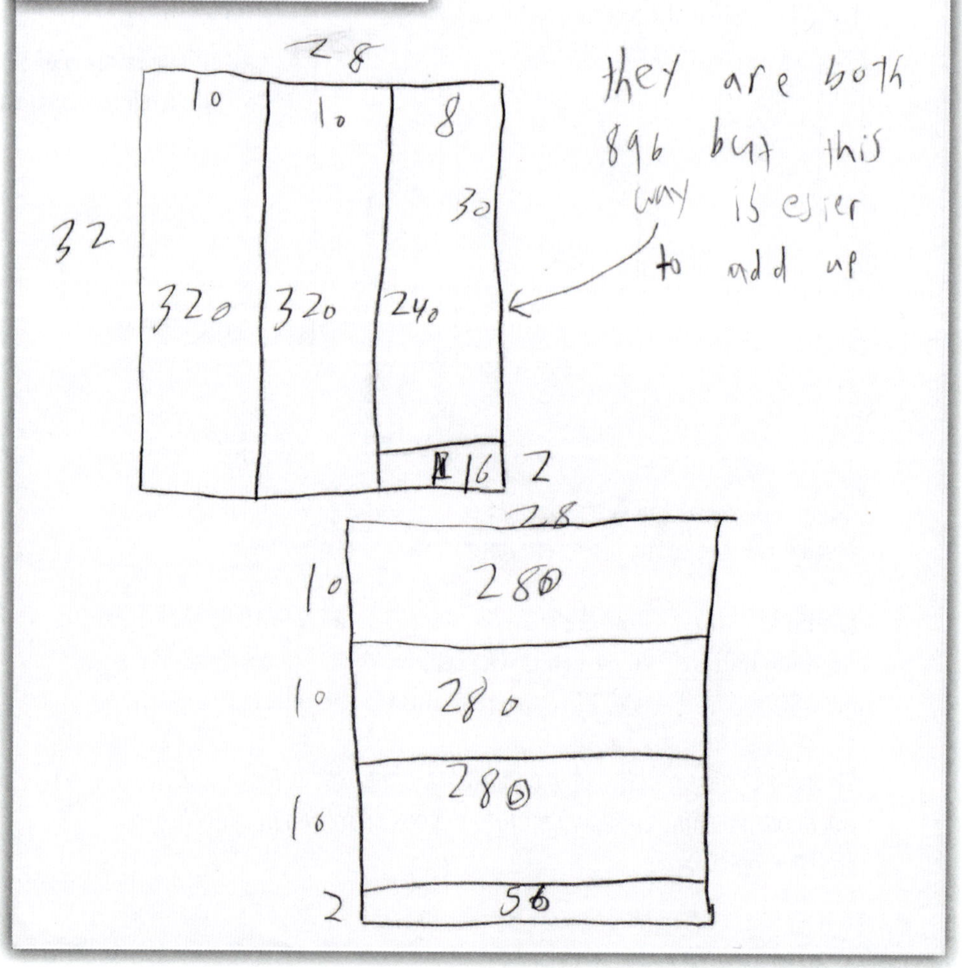

Notice and Name Concepts Students Are Discovering

You may observe students playing around with interesting ideas that they're unaware of or that just haven't come up in their learning yet or that are well outside the scope of your curriculum. It can be exciting for them to learn that their play has uncovered something fancy.

> **A pair of fourth graders are exploring fractions by playing with origami paper.**
>
> **Nahirul:** No matter how many times we fold it in half, we'll never get to zero. I mean, it's just going to keep on getting tinier.
>
> **Edmon:** That also means there's an infinite amount of numbers between zero and one.
>
> **Nahirul:** Whoa. Exploding head.
>
> *They're certainly not ready for precalculus, but it might just feel exciting to know that their heads are exploding because this is a big idea!*
>
> **Me:** You know, there's actually a word in math to describe the idea that you can get closer and closer to a number and still never get there. It's called a limit.

Create Opportunities to Explore and Build Understanding Collaboratively

You may see students across the room from one another, or two students who rarely choose to work together, exploring similar ideas in their play. By inviting them to share and discuss their observations and questions, you enable them to put their ideas into words. They may also inspire one another to create something new together out of the separate discoveries they've made.

> **Eric and Suria have both, completely separately, been collecting roots and making webs of words in Project Time.**
>
> *I have a feeling that by working together, they may push one another's thinking and make discoveries they wouldn't if they kept working separately.*
>
> **I tap Eric's shoulder and ask him to follow me over to where Suria is working. I lay his webs on the table.**

Fifth graders look for common elements in words as they plan an independent inquiry into word derivations.

> **Me:** Did you even know you were both doing this? It's up to you, but I'm thinking you could come up with something amazing if you worked as thought-partners.
>
> **Suria:** Can we talk about it first?
>
> **Me:** Of course! I said it was up to you, and there's no rush to decide.

Be Ready to Provide Additional Resources

A student or group that seems to be pursuing a focus or following a line of inquiry might not know how to locate resources that could help them. It might not even have occurred to them to look for any. When you observe play and exploration that seem aimed in a particular direction, think about resources that will engage and inspire your students, such as videos, images, and articles online or texts in your classroom, school, or local library.

My sixth-grade classes are playing in the school's block room as we launch a study of Ancient River Valley Civilizations. Small groups are building settlements next to a strip of blue tape I've placed down the middle of the floor. One group is discussing where they will place various types of building.

Noah: How does the water get from the river to all the homes?

Sasha: Well, how did they do it back in the day?

First of all, I love that "back in the day" can be 10,000 years ago. More importantly, I have just heard a student-articulated need for information that can be found in texts we have in the classroom.

Me: Should we be bringing our book baskets in here when we have block room days?

Noah: Yes! Can we go get them now?

Encourage Students to Explore Patterns They Have Found

Some students are drawn to patterns. It's exciting to stumble upon an apparent coincidence and wonder if it's actually a *thing*. Exploring these to figure out whether they're actual patterns or just blips leads to new knowledge for children and Nobel laureates alike. Students who have identified patterns may benefit from support or encouragement in finding meaning behind the pattern; Do they have a theory or conjecture? Or possibly a statement that goes, "Usually X, but sometimes Y"?

> **A student has a list of numbers on her paper. On first glance I don't see how they are related.**

Me: What are you finding out?

Sarah: My dad told me the digits of multiples of nine add up to nine, like eighteen and twenty-seven, but I was wondering about three- or four-digit numbers? Will they still add up to nine?

Me: Will they?

Sarah: So, kind of. Mostly they've been adding up to nine, but sometimes they add up to eighteen, and then *those* digits add up to nine.

She's beginning to identify a pattern, but it's not simple; she seems to need more data. I wonder if exploring the irregularity of the pattern will lead her to a conjecture.

Me: Will this always happen? What do you need to do to find out?

Sarah: Hmm. I think I need to keep trying bigger and bigger multiples of nine. For instance, 9,999. The digits add up to thirty-six, and those add up to nine, but I feel like I need more.

Invite Students to Document and Share Their Discoveries

Documentation is certainly not essential to the activity, and it does require an additional investment of time and management of more materials. The benefits are substantial, though. First, students become deeply engaged in documenting their playful explorations. They plan, organize, and compose in much the same way we encourage them to do as writers, and they are able to articulate interesting ideas. Second, without this step, you are the only one who gets to see and hear about what all the kids in the class are discovering. With a poster share or gallery walk, the whole community gets to learn from all its members. You can pull out some chart paper or large construction paper and support students in sharing their findings with an audience.

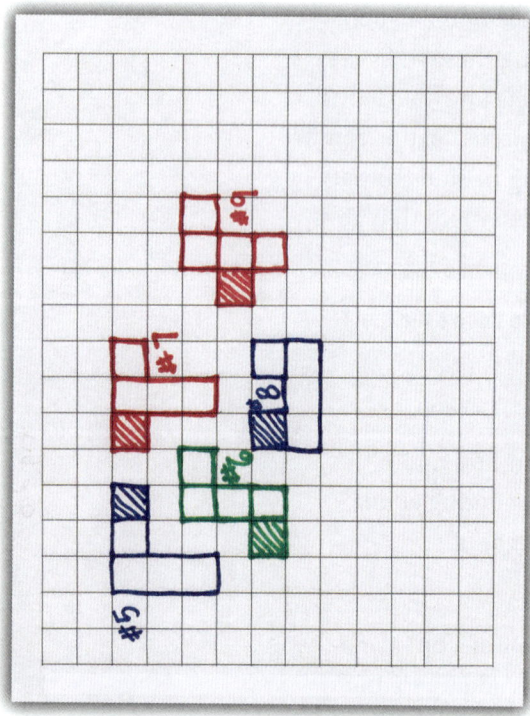

These students' quest to identify all possible pentominoes started randomly, but they soon realized they needed a system.

A pair of students is playing with square tiles to figure out how many possible different pentominoes can be made with five tiles. They have a line of five tiles. I watch as they slide one tile from the end of the line into a different position and then build a new line of five. They repeat the process of moving a single tile and recreating the prior pentomino.

Me: This looks interesting.

Ella: We were having trouble knowing if we had made a new one or if we had just made one we already had, but flipped or rotated.

Johan: Yeah, so we started over. We decided to start with a line and just move one tile at a time and keep checking every time if it was the same as another one.

Ella: Like here, if we slide this over one space, we'll have the same thing but flipped, so it won't count.

They have developed a systematic method for exploring the question, which includes testing their results as they go. This way of thinking could benefit the whole class.

Me: This method is so clear and makes so much sense. Is there a way, when you make your poster, to show this process?

Their poster tells the story of how they found all the pentominoes and how they are sure they have found them all.

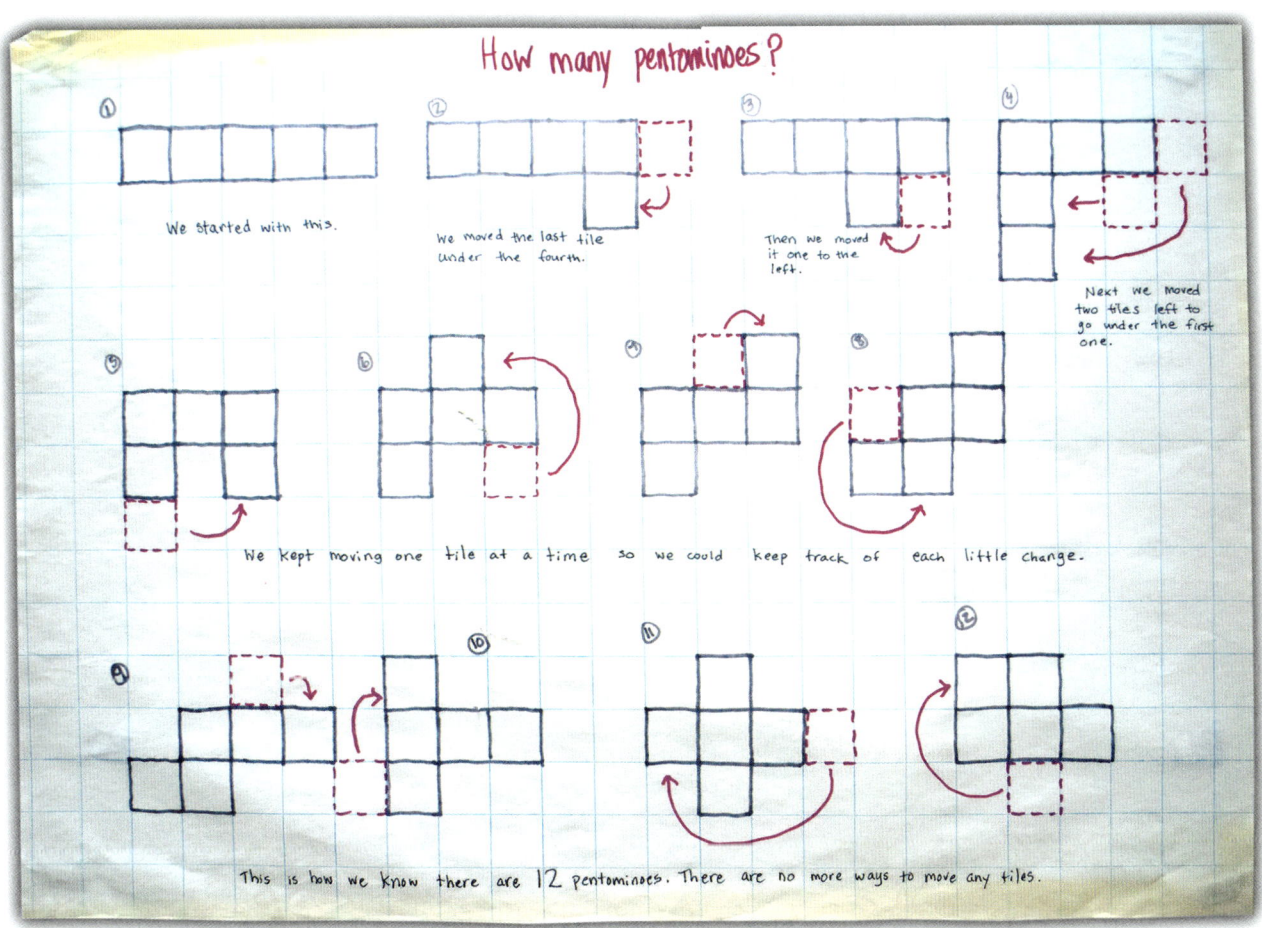

Their final poster illustrates how their system worked and offers convincing proof that they have found all the pentominoes.

Clean Up

Inevitably when children play, things need to be cleaned up when they are finished. Even small things like cleanup can be an opportunity to involve students in the decision-making process. In situations that involve familiar materials, it makes sense to follow familiar procedures for cleaning up. However, when using materials in a new combination, and especially when you're engaging in an exploration over multiple sessions, you'll need a new arrangement. As you stop the class to give a five-minute warning, suggest that students consider or discuss the fairest and most efficient way to clean up and get ready for the next part of the day. Some things to consider are:

- ★ Will the regular routine work?
- ★ Are there new materials or tools, which need to be put away in different places?
- ★ Do students or groups need a place to store work in progress?

If students have different ideas, such as cleaning up individually versus dividing up the work, try both and discuss how they worked in the reflection discussion.

With certain materials—ones that are messy or delicate perhaps—you might have an established cleanup procedure that has always worked for you. In this case you can simply explain it to the students. Even when you're not giving them much of a choice, however, you can still craft your language in a way that lets students know they are an integral part of class decisions. For example, you might say, "This is the way I have found it works best to clean this stuff up. If we come up with any helpful tweaks, let's write them down."

Reflect

Although reflection is not a necessary component of pure, free play, it is essential to playful classroom experiences. During reflection time, students look for meaning in their play and begin to find the words to articulate it. Reflection is also a powerful way to strengthen the learning community. Students might find different kinds of meaning in these explorations; some might be most affected by the new freedom they felt to take risks, and others will be moved more by some new understanding they developed about an academic concept. Students might consider how their own actions and decisions influence their individual work processes and learn more about themselves as learners. As

A Framework for Play in School

they think, write, and/or talk about their play, they solidify their own learning and have a chance to learn from the whole community. The reflection may or may not involve actual products to share and can take many different forms.

MENU OF WAYS TO REFLECT	
Think and/ or write to yourself	Probably the simplest way to support reflection, this can be done privately or in preparation for a class or small-group discussion. You can give a wide-open prompt, such as, "How did it go today?" or a more focused prompt, such as, "Explain something you learned about pronouns." You can also offer a menu of prompts from which students can choose—whether to reflect on what they learned, how they learned it, or what they would change about the experience, for example.
Yes or no?	After everyone has played, you bring the class to the meeting area, where students remain standing. Designate one side of the room as "yes" and the other side as "no." As you ask questions, students move to the side of the room that reflects their thinking. From there, you can call on individual students to elaborate or have them elaborate with partners within the group. Possible questions include: ★ Did something surprise you today? ★ Did you find anything out by accident? ★ Did your thinking change about anything? ★ Was anything hard?
Swap meet	This is a structure I originally learned at Responsive Classroom training (Wilson and Hodges 2015). Have students write down a big takeaway they got from the exploration on a sticky note or small piece of paper. They then circulate in the classroom, mixing and mingling with one another to discuss their takeaways. After sharing their notes, they swap. This means that in every subsequent share after the first one, students are now relating other students' takeaways.

(continues)

MENU OF WAYS TO REFLECT *(continued)*

Gallery walk	Students don't always get to see the full range of what their classmates are doing. If they have documented their discoveries as part of the exploration, a gallery walk allows them to examine one another's work and comment on it. You could leave it at that or give them time to return to their own work with new ideas. Giving and receiving feedback, possibly making revisions as a result, will add depth to the reflection conversation. A possible additional step is for students to categorize the feedback they received as "helpful" or "not helpful" and try to articulate why. If you are working with students to give quality peer feedback, doing this a few times can support a shared definition of what makes it helpful.
Congress	When students create objects or products as part of an exploration, you may decide to include these in the reflection process. This could mean that everyone (or each group) briefly shares what they made or that you choose two to four pieces to focus on in more detail (you could choose or have the class vote on pieces they are curious about). Leave a few minutes for questions about the artifacts.
Documenting the learning	Separate from the question of documenting their own learning is the question of documenting learning for the whole class. Charts created *with* students and not just for them are more meaningful and carry more weight. When students see their own learning and discoveries as part of the collective knowledge, they invest more in the process. This could become a chart or a reference sheet or book, for example.

Create an Environment That Supports a Playful Mindset

The value of playful experiences is even greater when it happens in a classroom that supports a playful mindset *all the time*. A playful mind is a learning mind, and the tone of a classroom can have a powerful effect on students' mindsets. In particular, teachers' language patterns influence how students respond to difficulty, misconceptions (their own and those of peers), and conflict. Be a model of approaching your own and your students' work and learning as a process that sometimes needs adjusting along the way, calmly noticing and facing challenges or errors.

In addition to these language moves, it's also important to *avoid* "Guess what I want you to say" responses such as "Close but not quite"; "I can see how you think that, but no"; or "Can someone help Amber with this one?' The goal is to use our teacher language to keep possibilities open in students' minds.

As you enter the next section of this book, you'll find a "Framework in Action" chart for each type of play experience, including ways to angle your lean input for that kind of play and specific questions to support reflection.

Go forth and have fun! But don't hesitate to return to this section of the book to remind yourself of the thinking behind all that fun you're having.

PLAYFUL LANGUAGE PATTERNS

Take risks without emphasizing the outcome.	*I'm going to try this. I'm kind of nervous because I've never done it before but . . . here goes!* *Let's see . . . what if I try . . .*
Acknowledge student risks.	*That was brave, and it helped all of us. Thank you!*
Handle your own mistakes calmly.	*Oops, it looks like I added two groups of ten instead of three. I forgot the extra ten that came from here. OK, do-over.* *That's spelled with a C, not an S? Thanks! I get those mixed up sometimes. I'm working on it.*
Respond to incorrect answers with curiosity.	*How did you come up with that?* Usually this will either enable students to correct errors: "Oops, I need to change my answer. I did 6 × 4 = 28 in the second step." Or it will help you diagnose the problem: She's confused about the order of operations.
Probe into misconceptions.	*Can you say more about that?* The answer may reveal that there is no misconception at all, but a difficulty in articulating a complicated thought. If there is a misconception, you'll be able to address it either right then or later. *Oh, I get it! You were imagining a train conductor, but this is about an orchestra conductor!*
Take revision for granted as part of doing or making anything.	*That didn't go as planned, but I can see exactly what I need to change next time.* *I'm glad I tried adding that in. I want to keep some of it but take this part back out.* *After reading this I completely changed my mind.*
Highlight student revisions.	*I notice you rearranged the paragraphs. Tell us how you decided to do that.* *You tried this first by drawing an open array, but then went to a different strategy. What made you do that?*
Use a "do-over" as a redirection.	*I think there's a more appropriate way to express that thought. Let's erase that, like it never happened, and you can have a do-over.* *If I'm already talking to someone, I want you to wait for a pause and say, "Excuse me." I'm going to talk to Eman again and you take a do-over.*

KINDS OF PLAY

How can activities we associate with play transform academic learning?

MAKING AND BUILDING Making and building things brings energy to content learning. In using their hands and minds to manipulate materials to explore possibilities or solve problems, students become motivated to learn what they need to know to realize their visions.

LANGUAGE Many children enjoy manipulating sounds and words, inventing new words, and learning more sophisticated or specific ways to say things. Playing with language supports brain elasticity and also brings fun (and therefore engagement) to topics that might feel tedious.

EXPLORATORY Children engaged in exploratory play—using their physical skills and senses to find out what things feel like and what can be done with them—are natural learners and sense makers.

PRETEND/FANTASY As children grow, their imaginations and their play become increasingly complex. Whether acting out actual events or engaging in fantasy play, children are able to explore questions and demonstrate learning in ways we wouldn't see in other tasks or activities.

SOCIAL Hanging out, bantering, and goofing around are forms of social play that contribute to the development of social competence. As children get older, they increasingly rehearse for adulthood in their play. In this way, children try on different ways of being.

PHYSICAL There are ways to welcome full-body movement into the academic process. Physical play can support cooperation and awareness of others as well as coordination and balance. Movement breaks and energizers wake up tired brains, ease transitions, provide an outlet for pent-up energy, and stimulate creativity. Improv games hone attention and listening skills. All of these are important for learning.

GAMES WITH RULES Children create structures or rules to guide much of their play but also enjoy games that come with a set of rules. Most of the play experiences in this book do not fall into this category, but it can be fun to adapt a familiar game, such as *Jeopardy!*, to content learning.

MATERIAL PLAY

*Often the hands will solve a mystery that
the intellect has struggled with in vain.*
—Carl G. Jung

My fourth-grade class is about to embark on a unit of study in geometry. Before formally launching the unit, I set aside a few days of math time for my students to play with a set of assorted plastic polygons and see what they can discover. I use the time to observe them closely, seeing what they do and don't know and what they're ready for academically.

As I survey the room, I see that two students have decided to start with a single shape, gathering a bunch of green rhombuses. Nina says, "Look, it's a star! Six of these all meet in a point in the middle."

Isa looks at the arrangement, tracing her finger in a circle around the point where the shapes meet. "So . . . that's 360° . . . ," she says. Picking up where Isa trails off, Nina adds, "So, each angle is, um, 60°." Isa starts to rearrange the shapes, wondering aloud, "Can the big angles all meet in a point?"

After creating the new arrangement, Isa exclaims, "They can! These ones are 120°! Look it looks like a 3-D box." Looking at the shapes, Nina concludes,

"The pointy angles are half the wide ones." As if to confirm this, Isa layers one rhombus over two others, saying, "Ooh, look!"

 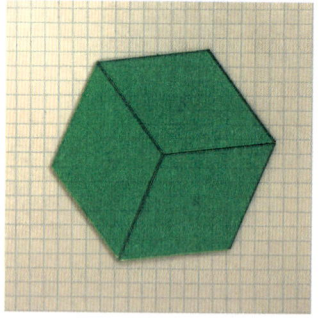 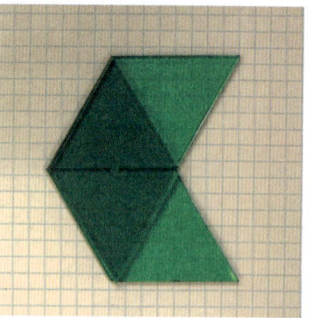

Nina then suggests getting more shapes to see what else they can figure out by arranging and layering. By the third day, they have created a poster explaining their findings.

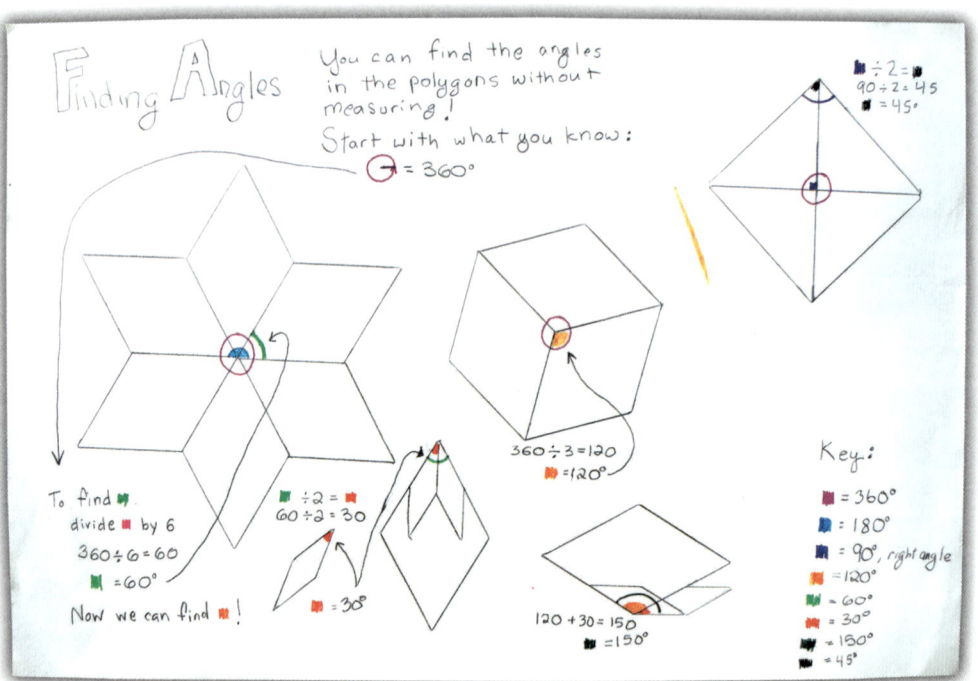

As I watched my students play with these manipulatives, I was struck again by this simple fact: Children want to learn. For us as teachers, it often doesn't feel that way. It seems like our students "just" want to play. Yet we know that play *is* learning. Over the three days they explored with polygons,

I saw my students demonstrating many of the mathematical practices defined by New York State Next Generation Mathematics Learning Standards and even meeting some of the standards for mathematical content the unit was meant to teach them.

NEW YORK STATE NEXT GENERATION STANDARDS: MATH PRACTICES

- Make sense of problems and persevere in solving them.
- Reason abstractly and quantitatively.
- Construct viable arguments and critique the reasoning of others.
- Model with mathematics.
- Use appropriate tools strategically.
- Attend to precision.
- Look for and make use of structure.
- Look for and express regularity in repeated reasoning.

© 2017 NYSED. Used with permission.

NEW YORK STATE NEXT GENERATION STANDARDS: MATH CONTENT

- Recognize angles as geometric shapes that are formed wherever two rays share a common endpoint, and understand concepts of angle measurement.
- Recognize an angle is measured with reference to a circle with its center at the common endpoint of the rays, by considering the fraction of the circular arc between the points where the two rays intersect the circle. An angle that turns through $\frac{1}{360}$ of a circle is called a "one-degree angle," and can be used to measure angles.
- Recognize angle measure as additive. When an angle is decomposed into nonoverlapping parts, the angle measure of the whole is the sum of the angle measures of the parts. Solve addition and subtraction problems to find unknown angles on a diagram in real-world and mathematical problems.
- Draw points, lines, line segments, rays, angles (right, acute, obtuse), and perpendicular and parallel lines. Identify these in two-dimensional figures.
- Identify and name triangles based on angle size (right, obtuse, acute).
- Recognize a line of symmetry for a two-dimensional figure as a line across the figure such that the figure can be folded along the line into matching parts. Identify line-symmetric figures and draw lines of symmetry.

© 2017 NYSED. Used with permission.

What Is Material Play?

In Material Play, students have a period of time to delight in working freely with materials, without any pressure to answer a question or figure anything out (though they most certainly will figure things out). Not having a goal, at least for a little while, makes it easier for students to take risks and to revise without angst. Students may make discoveries about the materials themselves or develop concrete schema for abstract concepts they're on the verge of learning. A key focus of this kind of play experience is the communication between the hands and the brain. Through manipulating materials and seeing the results, students make cognitive connections. Playing with materials develops facility, understanding, and specific expertise as students learn what various materials are good at doing.

As students playfully explore and discuss their discoveries with materials, your role as a teacher is active, but not prescriptive. You're taking note of what they're doing, making, or discovering and offering lean input. You're figuring out what they do and don't know. And you're learning things about your students that you would never learn if they were all doing the same thing at the same time.

Material Play is the simplest kind of play experience you can offer, and yet it often yields amazing results. Students can discover a lot exploring with materials in just a single period, or you can extend the play time across a few days or revisit it a couple of times throughout a unit, depending on your purpose and what you observe of students' learning. And because Material Play provides multiple entry points into content, engaging in it helps students build confidence. More than any other time in life, in the tween and early teen years, children seem to exaggerate others' abilities and their own shortcomings, but Material Play can level the playing field in terms of who feels "good at school" and who feels "bad at school."

The bottom line is when students have had a chance to explore and experiment with materials first through play, they are more adept at using them purposefully for academic reasons later. Allowing a small amount of time for this kind of playful engagement will buy you more and better instructional time in the long run.

Material Play

COMMON CLASSROOM MATERIALS

- ✦ **General classroom tools**
  - Individual dry-erase boards and markers
  - Sticky notes
  - Colored pens or pencils
  - Highlighters
  - Laptops and tablets
  - Apps
- ✦ **Construction materials**
  - Blocks
  - Legos
  - Cardboard boxes
  - Those big random bags of fabric, carpet samples, buttons, and other stuff that appears in seldom-opened school closets and basements
- ✦ **Art materials**
  - Drawing and painting media
  - Collage supplies
  - Adhesives
  - Sizes and shapes of paintbrushes
- ✦ **Math materials**
  - Measuring tools, such as rulers or protractors
  - Compasses
  - Plastic hand mirrors (these came in my math toolkit, for assessing symmetry, but we use them for all kinds of things)
  - Manipulatives of any sort (plastic polygons, pattern blocks, attribute blocks, snap cubes, base-ten blocks and, of course, Cuisenaire rods)
  - Math games
  - Number cubes and polyhedrons (We used to call these *dice*, but that word is associated with gambling, apparently.)
  - Grid or graph paper
- ✦ **Science materials**
  - Measurement tools, such as pan balances, scales, thermometers
  - Colored lenses
  - Magnets
  - Different kinds of solid or liquid materials
  - Blocks, ramps, and balls
  - Minerals or kinds of dirt and soil
  - Items collected in nature
  - Microscopes

Consider all the common classroom materials students might use during the year.

Consider It

Playful exploration with materials can support students' learning in three main ways:

- ★ when you need to *establish management* for materials you'll be using routinely in the classroom
- ★ when you want students to *explore the potential* of the materials
- ★ when you want students to *discover concepts*.

Each of these purposes requires slightly different invitations, playful experiences, and reflections, and a single activity may benefit the class in more than one of these ways, or one purpose may lead to another. For example, when my students played with dry-erase surfaces to establish management guidelines, they also discovered a lot of potential academic uses for the surfaces. Keeping your *main* purpose in mind, however, will help you plan and carry out engaging sessions of Material Play, so let's consider each one now.

Establish Management

Do you ever find yourself thinking, "I'm a little afraid to pull out these materials because it might lead to chaos. They're *fun*, and I just know students will be tempted to play with them." Nobody wants to be a wet blanket, but you also know that to get the learning benefits, students need to use materials in a certain way, which happens *not* to be the way they'll most want to use them. You don't have to choose sanity over effective teaching, though! Just take a class period, give stuff out, and invite students to play with the materials before they're expected to use them a certain way or to achieve a certain outcome.

If you know from experience a material might be difficult to manage, or if you suspect it might have more versatility or utility than you're imagining, this kind of playful exploration is fairly open-ended and will help you identify predictable behaviors you want to avoid and tendencies you want to encourage. Your students might even discover a way to learn with the materials that your adult mind hadn't considered.

There are, of course, times when you'll just want to tell students your expectations or engage them in a quick discussion about the use of a material. For example, when most of my students were using mechanical pencils, I simply told them (based on what I had seen them doing), "You'll have to experiment with how much to click out the lead and how hard you can press in order not to break it off, but please don't keep on clicking it way out or pull out the whole piece! We need these pencils to last." You don't need a period of play to figure out every management situation.

Explore Potential

When students play with paints, magnets, microscopes, apps, and other materials, they learn what these materials can do and what their limitations are. They get a feel for how to use them without the added pressure of a grade or having to accomplish something specific, and they're freed to take risks and see where their explorations might lead them. If you want students to experience the full range of what a set of materials can do, introducing them before students need to use them in a unit or project will help them learn to use the materials more purposefully and with less frustration.

Since the goal is finding out how to work with the materials, you'll invite students to be creative and to try things purely to see what happens (the materials must be safe, of course; you wouldn't put out bleach and ammonia, for example). As students playfully explore, certain kinds of expertise may emerge. For example, in exploring possible apps for documenting a work process, some students may become experts in adjusting images while others become experts in making short videos with voice-overs. Knowing who's good at what supports your community and lets students be resources for one another (instead of always looking to you). Students might list on a chart what they can help others do, or you might create a shared pictorial guide of best practices for using the material.

Discover Concepts

A third reason you might engage students in Material Play is to create conditions that lead to exciting conceptual discoveries like those my students made as they played with the plastic polygons. Play has been shown to support cognitive development by providing concrete references of abstract concepts. Between third and eighth grade, school places an enormous burden on children to master abstract concepts, often without enough support to truly understand them. For example, as children progress through school, math concepts get increasingly harder to attach to concrete experiences. It seems easier, frankly, to teach that when dividing one fraction by another, one simply flips one of the fractions over and multiplies across. But why? Why does this work? For the many people who have not (yet) developed a capacity for visualizing these ideas, a chance to let their physical senses do the learning makes a huge difference. This is where one of the most elegant and satisfying features of Material Play comes in—it's inherently differentiated, perfectly tuned to the needs of a wide variety of students.

The key is, when you use Material Play to discover or deepen students' understanding of concepts, your focus shifts from the materials themselves to *how* children explore them. You might even say the material you choose is, um, immaterial. I first invited students to explore fractions through origami paper because I had a lot of it. I could have used grid paper or strips of paper and the students would still have discovered a lot.

Whatever materials you choose to use, students almost always strengthen their talk and collaboration skills as they discover concepts through Material

In choosing materials, you might need to consider how many variables to include; having too many to experiment with all at once can muddy the results. For example, if you want students to explore how colors mix with tempera paints, they may gain more useful experience by starting with just primary colors one day and adding black and white the next day.

Play. When they put ideas into words that a peer can understand, students see the learning that's developing inside the fun. Considering the materials, the students, and your purposes, you'll have to decide whether an exploration is collaborative from the beginning or whether you want students to start out individually and let collaborations form (or not) organically.

Documentation is important, so as soon as students start talking about their discoveries, put out large pieces of paper and markers so they can record them. Be sure to remind students there is an authentic purpose and audience for their documentation. "This is so exciting! Nobody is doing quite the same thing! I'm wondering what we should do to document this so that everyone can see what everyone else is discovering."

Imagine It

Although the possibilities for Material Play are almost endless, I've collected some of my favorites from my own classroom experience to highlight here. Remember that for any one of these materials, you might play with them purposefully to establish management, explore potential, or discover concepts, though often the play will naturally serve more than one purpose. You might want to try some of these explorations, and I hope they'll give you ideas for other explorations with other materials.

Dry-Erase Surfaces

I have seen dry-erase surfaces change the way my students take risks and work with ideas across content areas. Somehow, it's easier to float an idea or try out a strategy when you can simply wipe away what doesn't work for you. And because people also love to draw, doodle, scribble, and play games on dry-erase surfaces, they are an ideal candidate for using play to coauthor management guidelines with students before using them for learning purposes. Another benefit is that students will likely come up with academic applications that hadn't occurred to you. This playful exploration works best when the surfaces are brand-new to students, and a single class period is generally enough time.

If you don't have dry-erase tables or walls in your classroom, you can cover the surfaces you do have with dry-erase material. Smooth vinyl works too, and can just be taped onto tables, though it will bubble and move around a little, and some very smooth school desks work as dry-erase surfaces without any additional treatment. Make sure you have enough dry-erase pens and some sort of erasers for every student.

This process for play applies to many other fun materials that support learning.

Ask students what they want to do with the dry-erase when they get a chance and invite them to suggest parameters. For example, you might ask:

★ *What kinds of things do you want to do with the dry-erase?* (Draw, play games like tic-tac-toe, make comics?)

★ *We want to make sure we can use these materials all year, so is there anything we need to think about in terms of how we treat the materials?* (We should replace the caps when we're done. We shouldn't press too hard.)

★ *Is there any chance that someone could get offended or hurt by something a classmate does?* (If you draw a picture that makes fun of someone, like making them with a huge nose, that could hurt their feelings. We shouldn't write mean things about people.)

Students will not be short of ideas for how to explore the materials playfully. Once they get started, observe how they engage with the activity, and with one another. Much of what you see will inform the management guidelines for future use of the dry-erase materials. Remember that you're also part of the learning community, though, and it's nice to remind them that adults like to play, too. Think aloud to share your own inquisitive approach about, for example, whether certain brands of markers work better than others or what happens when you go over one color with another.

After the entire play session is over, reflect with the class about what was fun, what students discovered, and the best method for clean up. Ask them to share discoveries, advice, and whether or not it's necessary to create a chart of tips or "rules." If you want to post guidelines, rather than just discuss and agree to them, you might add another fifteen minutes the following day to review them.

If students want the materials to last, and if they want the environment to feel emotionally safe, they will agree to the management rules you establish *together*. If the same rules are simply presented to them by an adult, students will either be compliant (and possibly resentful) or they'll try to hide as they do whatever it is they actually want to do. Either way, they lose their agency as members of a learning community and all sense of play is lost.

Student-developed guidelines for dry-erase table surfaces

> Dry-Erase Table Agreements:
> - Press lightly with pens
> - Draw and write appropriate things. (If you're not sure, don't do it. Or ask.)
> - Leave other people's drawing and writing.
> - Treat the surface gently.

Bulletin Boards

Working together to decide how you might use the blank space on a bulletin board is a powerful way to build community and increase students' ownership of their learning. Students can help curate bulletin boards for both viewers outside the classroom and learners inside, considering what is most important and helpful to them.

Early in the year, as you share and reflect in content areas, engage students in conversations about how bulletin boards are typically used and what else might be possible. The goal is to invite students to think about the space with a playful mindset. You might ask:

★ *What has been helpful or important to display?*

★ *Can you imagine other possibilities for how we might use this space?*

★ *Do you have ideas for bulletin board content you could manage on your own?*

★ *How can we tell when it's time for something to come down?*

During lessons or share times, you might also ask whether a strategy, example of student work, reminder, or other idea should go on a bulletin board, or if you need to designate a board for a certain purpose.

Students use the bulletin board as a place to hold ideas or questions that can't be addressed right away.

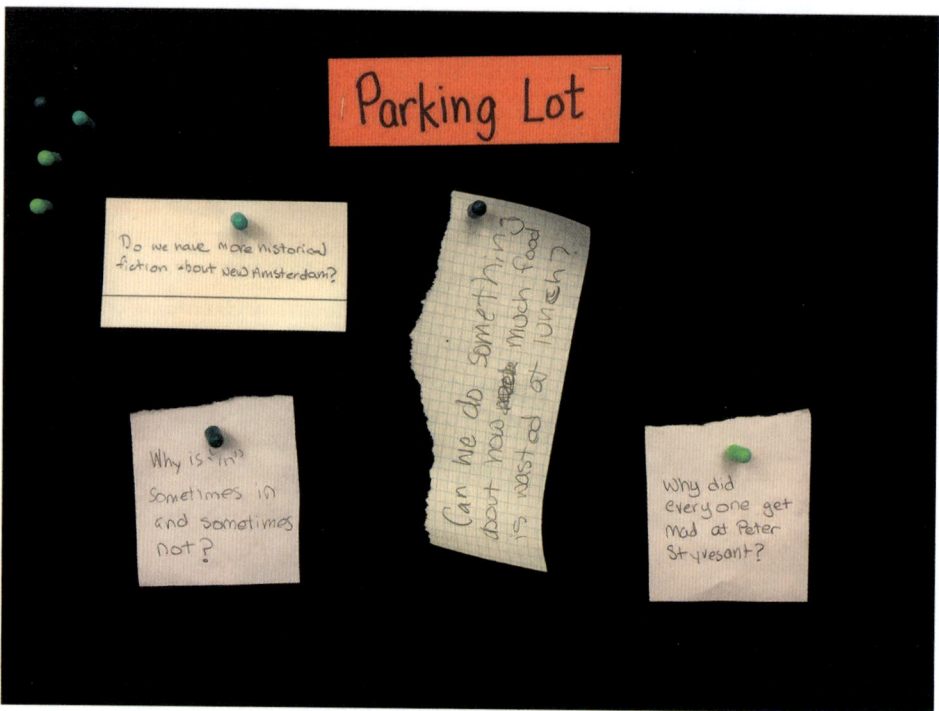

Material Play 53

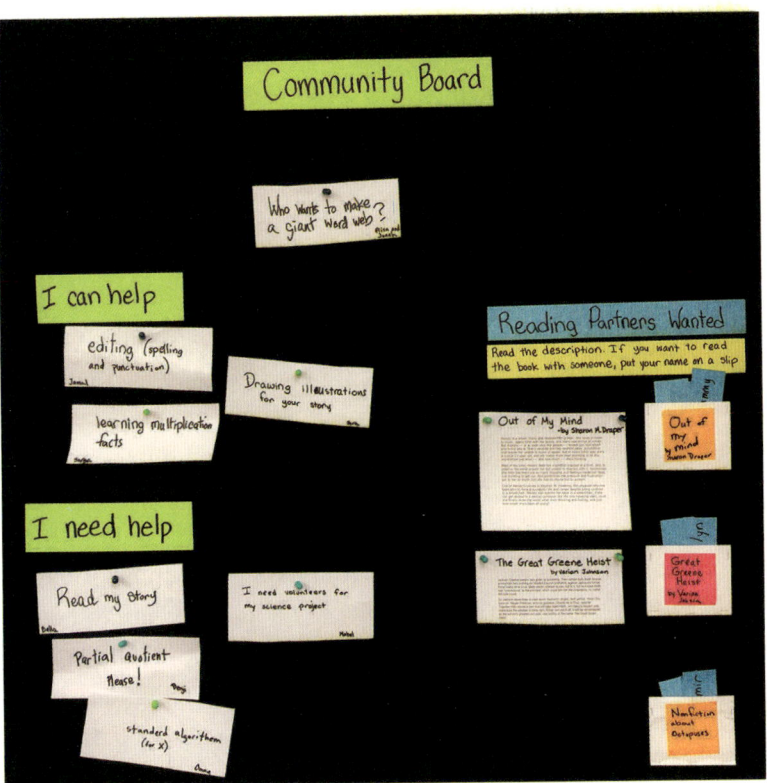

Students can post information such as book recommendations, helpful websites, tips for keeping organized, things they either need help with or are willing to help others with, and so on for classmates on a community resource board.

Students can show work in process (rather than finished). A board might feature, for example, a variety of notebook entries showing how different students approach their work, a set of connected entries showing how one student's work evolves, or some messy drafts showing how different students approach revision.

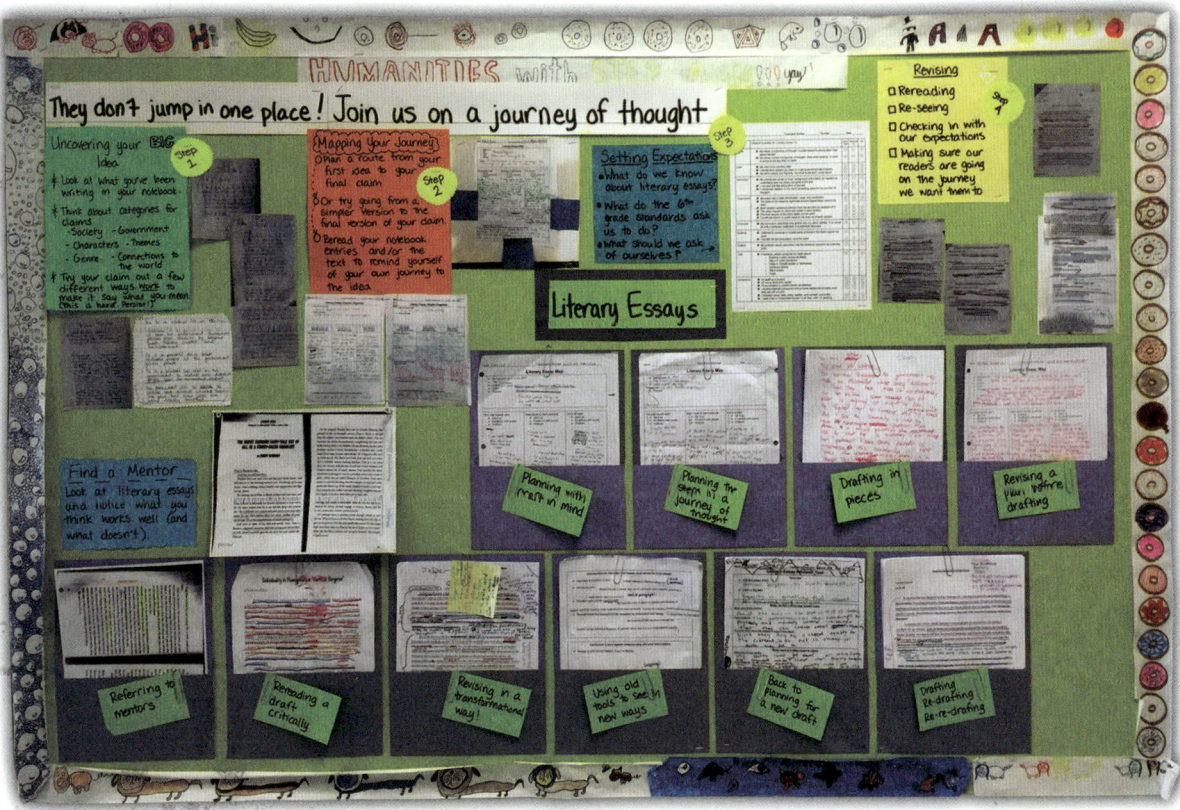

Play Attention!

Highlighters

Have you ever asked students to highlight while reading or color-code a draft and then been baffled at the variety of ways they come up with to do the *least helpful thing*? (I'm picturing, for example, the article or short story with 98 percent of the words highlighted.) Try to remember they're not "doing it wrong." They're approximating and, in doing so, telling us what they need to learn. When we tell students to highlight what seems most important, we assume they know what is most important and that this is static. But in fact, five out of five adults I surveyed indicate that they highlight differently depending on their purpose.

Students need time to explore and reflect on highlighting if they're going to learn to do so with purpose. By exploring and reflecting on the act of highlighting (rather than highlighting in service of an assignment) children may come to understand that, for example, people highlight because they intend to return to the text to find what they need easily, or that if they were to read the text for a different purpose, they might decide to highlight differently. An added benefit is that when you study their explorations with highlighters, you learn a lot about how students read.

Students' thoughts about highlighters lead to a couple of periods of playful inquiry.

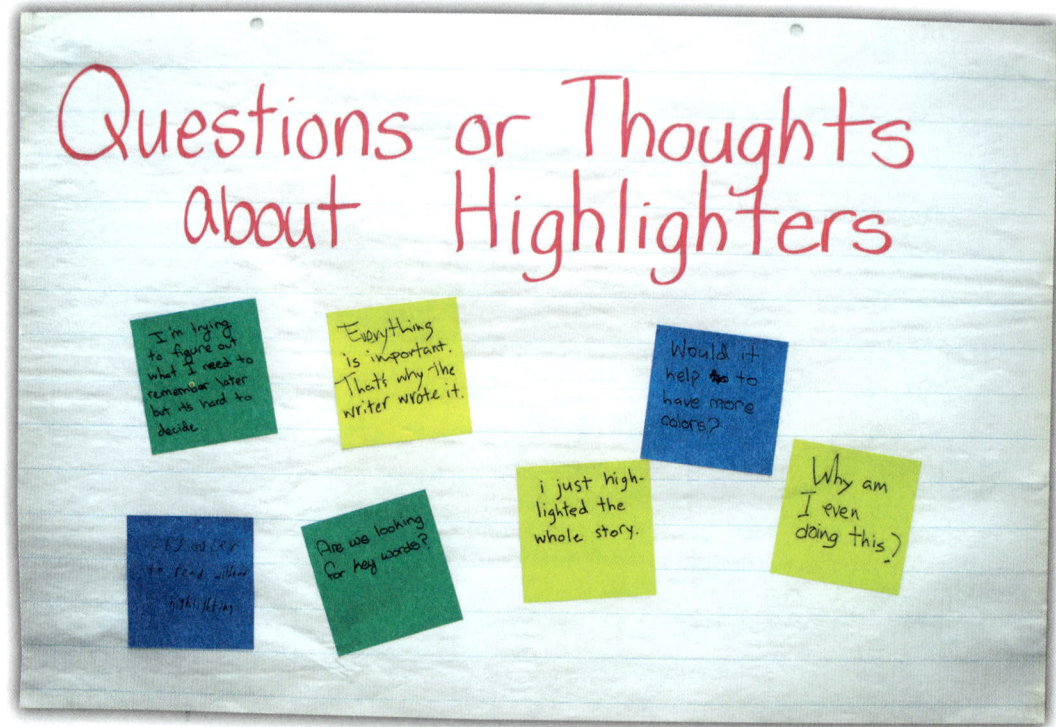

Invite students to join you in an inquiry into how highlighters can actually help them as readers. It can help to ask them what's been confusing or hard about reading with a highlighter if they've done it before. Starting with a text that is not too challenging, give the same text to the whole class and ask students to highlight what they think makes sense. This is a pre-assessment, for both you and the students, so it's intentionally open-ended. Choose a few different examples to discuss with the class, inviting students to name what they see. Then collect and chart students' questions or hypotheses about highlighting.

Once you have some general questions and thoughts about highlighting, you can enlist students to work in small groups to explore further. Some ways they might focus their inquiry include highlighting a text with attention to:

★ character development or change

★ relationships

★ author's craft

★ supporting an argument

★ answering a question.

In your final reflection, revisit your first chart with students, revising or refining it to create a brief list of tips for highlighting.

Although some students still prefer not to use highlighters at all, the ones who do have a much clearer sense of how to use them with intention.

This also works with colored pens for students who are exploring color-coding, in both reading and writing.

Art and Craft Supplies

I love giving students opportunities to incorporate visual information in their learning, but I feel horrible when they bring in projects they did at home and the vast diversity in resources, from money and materials to caregivers' time and attention, is more on display than the learning. When I want students to visually represent their learning (dioramas, collages, etc.), I give them time to work on these projects in class and I provide the same materials to all students.

Often, these projects are assessed, at least in part, by how effectively and intentionally materials have been used, and the appearance of the finished project matters to students, so experimenting with the materials first in lower-stakes ways makes sense. A few examples of explorations that require only a single class period are:

- ★ the different purposes for choosing zip ties, wire, or glue guns to connect dowels or sticks in a building
- ★ how glue sticks, double-sided tape, glue guns, and regular glue work on different surfaces
- ★ the effects of different sizes of brush and amounts of water on watercolor paint.

A student uses a hammer in a building project.

Student-made tips, advice, and precautions add to their sense of agency and ownership in the classroom.

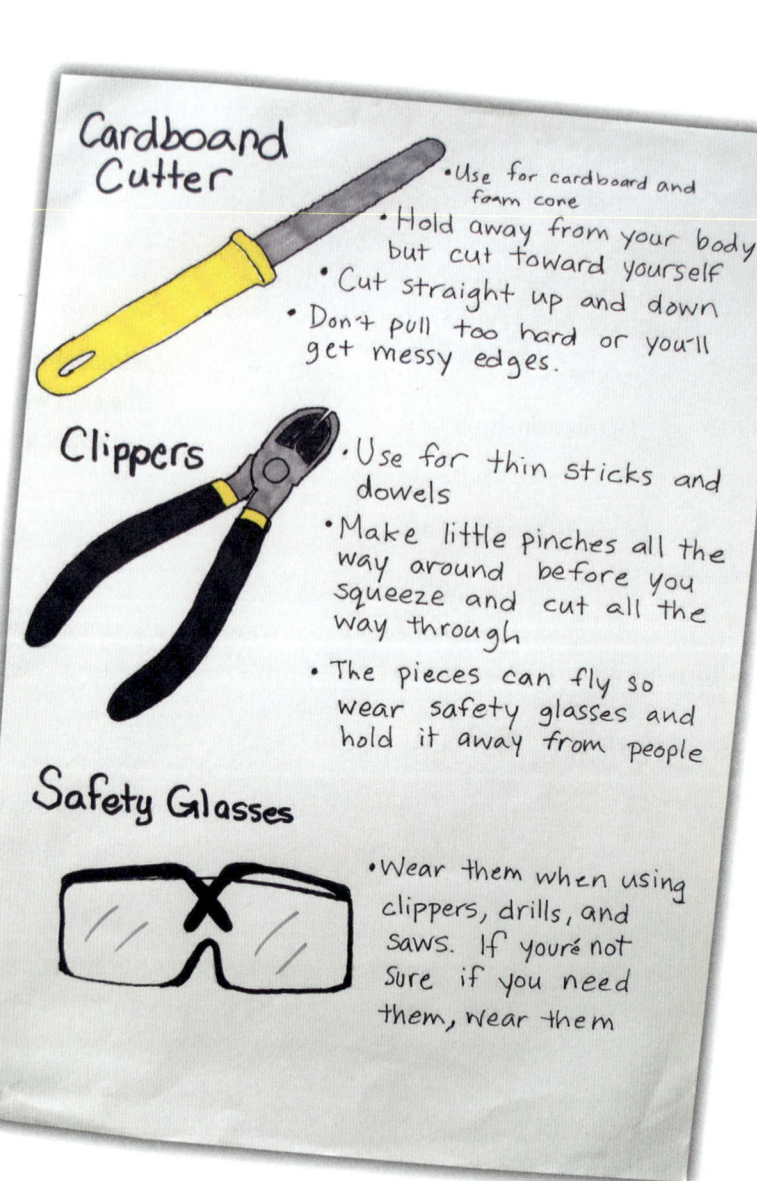

Science Tools and Materials

Material Play works well as a precursor to some science units, either in preparing students to use tools that can be tricky (like microscopes and pan balances) or in activating questions about a topic (like magnetism or electricity). Understanding how to use, adjust, and manipulate equipment is just as important as content learning. A period of playful exploration will reduce the amount of time you spend reminding or reteaching how to use those microscopes or pan balances. Also, it can be challenging to generate interest in some science topics, particularly when they are familiar and students think they know all about them. In such cases, a period of playful exploration can spark enthusiasm and an openness to the possibility of new learning.

With tricky equipment, such as a microscope, find out what students already know about it. For example, it magnifies things, it's meant for seeing things very close up, and so on. You might also give a minimal demonstration of careful handling to avoid damage. Then, invite students to look at a variety of things they are curious to see up close, turning the knobs, moving the mirrors, and otherwise exploring the effects of various adjustments on what they see. In the reflection conversation, give the academic or technical vocabulary when necessary, such as *lens* or *magnification*. Sometimes it's helpful to use their discoveries to create and label a diagram of the equipment.

When building interest in a material, such as magnets, try to allow for as many different ways to use it as possible. For example, put out bins of magnetic and nonmagnetic things, including nonferrous (nonmagnetic) metals, and different shapes or sizes of magnets. Then, invite students to play around with them. Some will want to

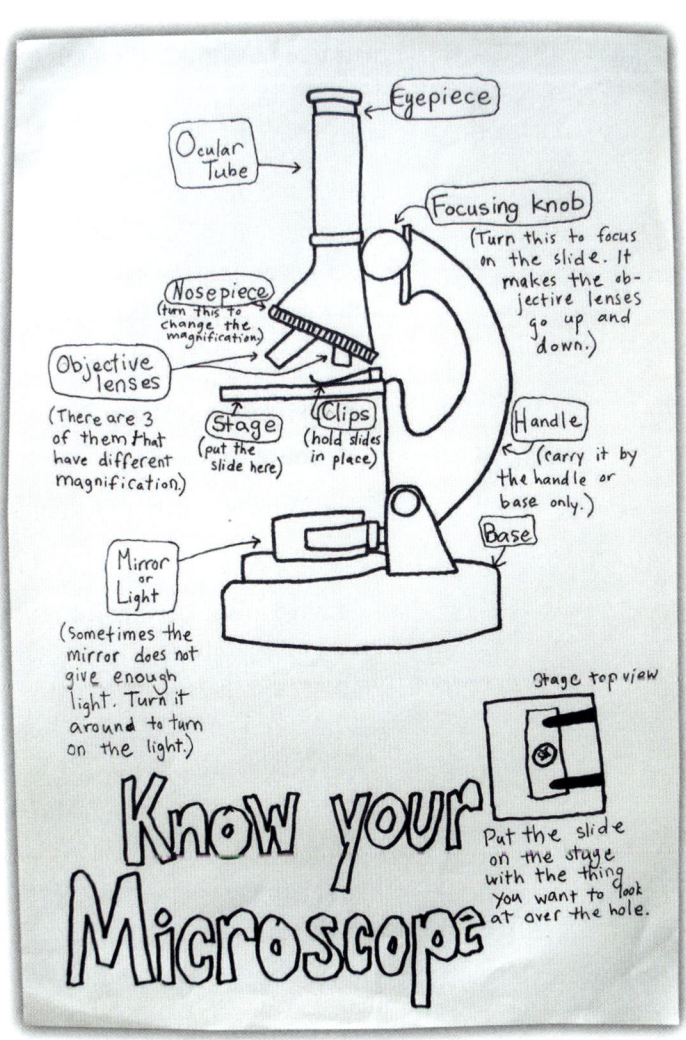

Advice coming from peers feels collaborative rather than prescriptive.

play with multiple magnets and explore questions such as how many can be stuck together? How does the attraction work? Why do they sometimes repel each other? Can I move a magnet by putting another one nearby? Can I put a magnet on the table and drag it around by sliding another one underneath the surface of the table? Why doesn't this always work? Does the size of a magnet indicate its power? Other students may incorporate the other materials into their experiments. What does and doesn't attract a magnet? Through how many layers of fabric or paper will a magnet "pull" another magnet? Do all the magnets have the same strength? Why do some metals stick and others don't? Does magnetism work through water? These concrete experiences will provide schema for later lessons, and they will also make it easier for students to focus during more guided experiments where they might otherwise have been distracted by how fun magnets are.

Globes and Map Projections

Globes and maps are fascinating. They represent, well, a *world* of possibilities, and exploring them can stand alone as its own playful inquiry or be part of a larger geography or earth science unit. The first time I decided to let students play with these materials, their questions fueled my plan. I'd heard them wondering:

- ★ Why are globes tilted?
- ★ How can it always be later to the east, and earlier in the west? Doesn't it have to start over somewhere?
- ★ Why is Greenland so big on some maps and not on others?
- ★ Why does Antarctica appear to have a flat edge on some maps?

I have found that giving students some extended time to examine and explore globes, talking about what they notice and wonder, yields questions that students are motivated to figure out how to answer. They learn about latitude and longitude, time zones, the international date line ("You mean there's a place where I could jump a few feet and it would be tomorrow? Or yesterday?"), cardinal directions, the relative sizes and locations of places, and more. This hands-on, minds-on kind of exploration yields so much richer thinking than reading a chapter in a textbook or completing a worksheet.

After some playful exploration with globes, you may then want to approach "the orange peel problem" of trying to create a flat representation of a spherical object. Using large paper or plastic sheets, students try to create flat maps that could cover their globes. This often leads to the question of accuracy versus ease of use, which leads to the question of purpose.

After looking at several different map projections, students had a better understanding of how different maps serve different purposes.

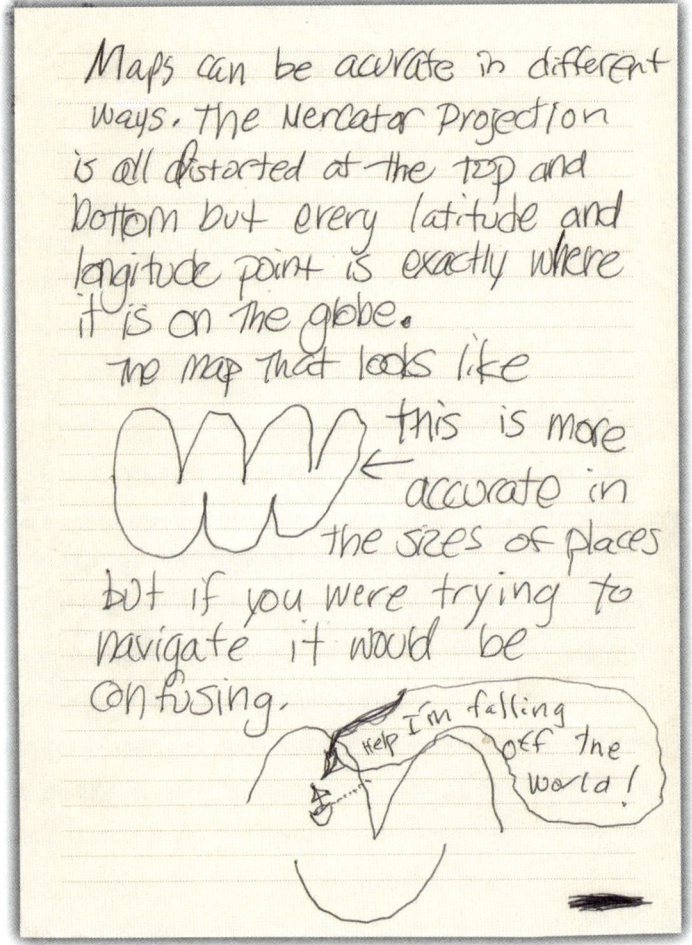

As a concrete way to understand the challenges of making a flat map of a spherical object, students tried to cover inflatable globes in paper.

Fractions

Many math curricula don't give children enough time to explore concepts such as fractions through concrete and pictorial means before expecting mastery at the abstract level. With some playful paper exploration—folding, marking up, cutting, and comparing—students can explore fractional relationships in a concrete and visual way. Origami paper supports understanding fractions in an area model, and strips of paper (pretending they only have length and not width) supports understanding in a linear model. Children at a more advanced level also benefit from this exploration; it is open-ended enough to allow students to learn what they are ready for.

To really build some conceptual understandings, this kind of play usually takes two to three math periods, and it requires more specific framing, which I'll demonstrate for you here. To get started, let students know that fractions make more sense and are easier to work with when you have a way of visualizing them. You might say something like:

> We've been learning about fractions, and sometimes it can be confusing to work with them when they're written down. It can be hard to remember or visualize what the numbers in the numerator and denominator mean. We're going to have a chance to play around with paper to see if it helps us discover new ways to think about fractions.

Demonstrate how this could look by showing students how to find some simple fractions using a piece of origami paper. You might use language like this:

> If I think of this square piece of paper as one whole, I can make halves by folding it into two rectangles. If I open it back up, you can see that each one is half of my whole—two halves. I can fold it again, making sure I match up the corners so it's even. When I unfold it this time, I have four fourths!

Think aloud to show your own inquisitive approach to what you're doing. For example,

> *This kind of makes me wonder what fractions I can make that are also square, just by folding. I tried, but I can't fold square halves. I can make halves that are triangles, though. I wonder if there's some kind of pattern to which fractions can be folded into which shapes. I just want to keep seeing what I can find out!*

Finally, offer any tips or guidelines that will help the exploration yield good results. For example, you might agree that one piece of origami paper will equal one unit. This will ensure that students all have the same point of reference when you're talking about fourths or halves or other fractions. If you need to consider different units, you can talk about it when it comes up.

You could also pose some questions that get students thinking about the exploration itself, and how it may benefit them as learners:

★ What's important to know about this kind of material? (It's square. Other shapes may lead to different discoveries.)

★ How can we organize our exploration to learn from it? (Some people may have a methodical approach planned out, whereas others may want to see where their questions and discoveries lead.)

As students go off individually or in partnerships, observe how they engage with the activity. Notice students who:

★ explore the part-to-whole relationship

★ explore the relationships between different fractions

★ explore equivalence

★ explore multiplying or dividing fractions

★ take risks with bigger or more awkward numbers

★ begin to get into advanced territory.

Play Attention!

As students begin making interesting discoveries in their fraction play, ask them, "How can you keep track of or document what you discover?" Students can make posters, guides, or slideshows, for example, incorporating pictures, numbers, words, or a combination of all three. Regardless of how you choose to reflect, it is helpful to have students write at least a brief description of what they learned.

Exploring fractions by manipulating concrete materials helps students build solid conceptual understanding of how fractions work.

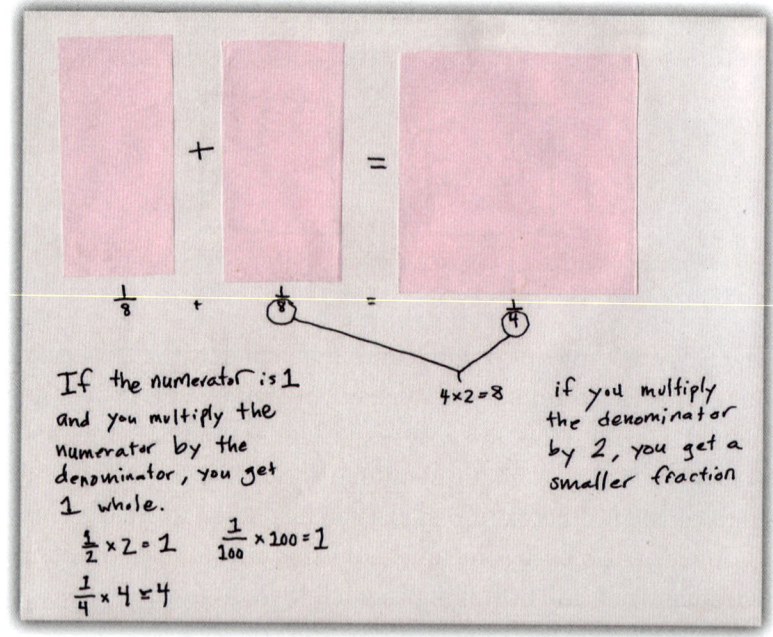

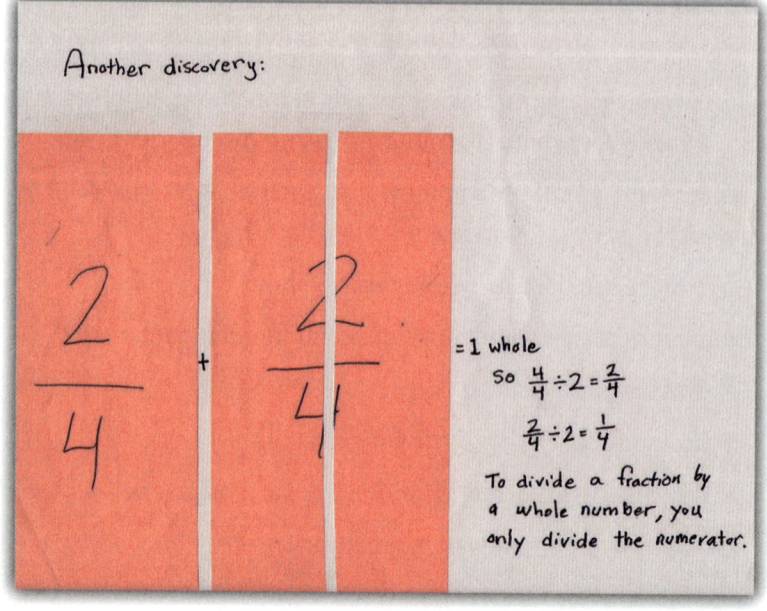

Plan It

Materials take center stage in these explorations and will be central to your planning. You might start with a problem of practice or a teaching objective, and then think about which materials will provide the best support for your students. You can also think about the materials you will be using across the year to support all kinds of learning.

Once you've decided which materials you'll explore, the first step in planning is to play with the materials yourself so you can predict how students may explore and the challenges they may encounter. Based on your experience, you can tweak the materials appropriately, and you might also come up with a list of possible questions or tips to use in various scenarios.

When using Material Play to establish management or gain facility with a particular material, the topic and material are tied together. However, when you want to use Material Play to support learning about abstract concepts, you have both the opportunity and the challenge to choose materials creatively that can give schema for what you'll be teaching. Following is a list of materials and concepts that work well together.

MATERIAL POSSIBILITIES FOR CONCEPT DISCOVERY

MATERIAL	POSSIBLE EXPLORATIONS
Large paper (sheets or rolls)	★ Nets of 3-D shapes (visualizing geometric solids as flat shapes that could theoretically be folded to create the solid) ★ Trying different art media or color mixtures
Grid paper (sheets, chart paper, or rolls)	★ Arrays (area model for multiplication, visual model for the distributive property) ★ Area and perimeter (relationship between the two, maximizing and minimizing area with given perimeter and vice versa, relationship between a unit and a square unit) ★ Scale (effects of scaling up or down on overall area) ★ Nets of 3-D shapes (grid lines may offer more support than plain paper and can lead to greater understanding of volume) ★ Surface area and volume (creating solids with grid paper copied onto card stock; looking at relationship between grid marks to visualize area and volume; relationship between a unit, square unit, and cubic unit) ★ Mapping (creating maps of known places to support more abstract understanding of scale, creating one-to-one topographical maps of clay landforms) ★ Place value (to hundreds or hundredths)

(continues)

MATERIAL POSSIBILITIES FOR CONCEPT DISCOVERY (continued)

Origami paper	★ Fractions (area model; equivalence; adding, subtracting, multiplying, and dividing fractions) ★ Area (relationship between area of square or rectangle to area of triangles within)
Paper strips or rolls	★ Fractions (linear model, equivalence, adding and subtracting fractions) ★ Decimals on a number line
Clear vinyl on a roll	★ Dry-erase surface ★ Creating a flat representation of a globe (try to cut a piece that covers the globe with as little overlap as possible, then trace the continents onto the vinyl with dry-erase pens) ★ Creating overlays to show change or inside versus outside
Globes and maps	★ Visualizing concepts such as time zones, seasons, poles (a flashlight is helpful) ★ Latitude and longitude ★ Projections and the reasons that different ones exist
Plastic polygons	★ Angle measure (individual angles and interior angle measure) ★ Fractions with area model ★ Areas of polygons

The Framework in Action for Language Play

INVITE

Invite students to discover as much about the material as they can or use the material as creatively as they can to discover new ideas: something that the teacher hasn't thought of, that's not in the curriculum (at least not for this grade), or that changes minds about something. The experience should be driven by your students' desire to discover, rather than pressure to get an answer.

★ *This is something that can help us in the classroom, probably in a lot of ways. Before we start using it as a learning tool, I wanted you to have a chance to play around with it. I need you to help me figure out some of the ways it can help us learn, and also if there are any rules or guidelines we should agree to so it lasts the whole year.*

★ *These can be fun tools, but sometimes I'm mystified about how to use them! I have come to suspect that there isn't really a single most helpful way. Do you want to help me figure out some tips?*

★ *We're going to be using this material in a project or unit soon. To get the most out of it, let's explore and experiment to see how it works and what it's really capable of.*

You might invite children to touch or hold the materials first, then consider questions like these:

★ *What do you most want to do with this? What do you want to try first?*

★ *What potential do you see here?*

★ *How could this be useful in class?*

★ *We use this a lot, but I wonder if there are applications we haven't thought of yet?*

If you suspect you need parameters to ensure safety and respect, consider questions like these:

★ *How can we avoid causing damage to our classroom, the materials, or ourselves?*

★ *Could someone get hurt physically or emotionally? How can we avoid that?*

★ *What's important to know about this material?*

(continues)

The Framework in Action for Language Play (continued)

PLAY

Observe

Look closely at what students do or make, watching how they use, arrange, or manipulate the materials, and listening to their conversations about it. Ask yourself questions like these:

★ *What are students doing that may get in the way of their later academic work?*

★ *Are they doing anything I didn't anticipate that might actually support later academic work?*

★ *What experiments are they trying?*

★ *Are they talking about what they find out? How?*

★ *Are they trying to achieve certain results or just seeing what happens?*

★ *Are they keeping track? How?*

★ *Do they seem hesitant even to use the materials playfully?*

★ *Are they working with a single variable or more (one shape, color, method, etc.)?*

★ *Do I see students working separately with a similar idea? Would a discussion or collaboration benefit them?*

★ *Is anyone forming conjectures or making generalizations?*

Photos are a particularly useful form of documentation for Material Play, especially if students erased, wiped away, or dismantled something without documenting it themselves. They're also handy if your class decides to make a guide on using the material.

Provide Lean Input

Offer questions or thoughts that further students' in their own lines of inquiry or scaffold a discovery they're on the verge of making. As they explore, ask questions such as:

★ *What if you . . . ?*

★ *If you wanted to _____, what could you try?*

★ *What other ways can you try?*

★ *What do you notice about how _____, (pieces, colors, numbers, etc.) work together?*

★ *Do you want to work with someone else who's exploring a similar question?*

★ *Is there a pattern? Does the pattern exist with different variables?*

★ *Does this always work? When does or doesn't it?*

★ *How could you document this for future reference or to share with the class?*

Try to enjoy their joy. It can be beneficial for you to get to play a little, too, and for students to see you as a model of curiosity. Especially if you find yourself wanting to lead students in a certain direction, going there with your own playful exploration can satisfy that urge.

The Framework in Action for Language Play *(continued)*

REFLECT

Whether you reflect purely in conversation or also in writing, some possible questions to include are:

- ★ *What was fun? Interesting? Surprising?*
- ★ *What did you find out?*
- ★ *What did you find out by accident?*
- ★ *Are you thinking of using this material in a particular way for a particular purpose?*
- ★ *Should this be available for free play or to use whenever we have any kind of free time?*
- ★ *When/how do you think this material could be useful in class?*
- ★ *What expectations should we set?*
- ★ *What parameters should be in place? Expectations? Norms?*
- ★ *Do we need to post these for a while, or will we just remember them?*

If students have created documents of their learning, you might consider having them do a gallery walk and comment on one another's notes and discoveries. You might also ask questions like these to consider how you can document learning for the whole class:

- ★ *How should we share our collective new knowledge?*
- ★ *Would it be helpful to know who the class experts are in using this material in different ways?*
- ★ *Do we need to post our expectations or tips for using this material for a while, or will we just remember them?*

LANGUAGE PLAY

Do not keep children to their studies by compulsion but by play.
—Plato

I'd like to give credit to my first fourth-grade class for inventing Language Play. Like many teachers before me, I sensed a need for some teaching around how grammar—the structures according to which we use language to communicate—works. In the middle of a conversation about parts of speech, my students kindly and patiently revealed to me that grammar had always bored them and that they saw little point in being able to identify parts of speech.

I pictured myself as a child, floundering in a swirl of worksheets. Circle all the pronouns! Change the adjectives to adverbs! Underline the compound verbs! Ooh, it's a crossword puzzle of irregular plurals!!

Just as a creepy clown was entering my mental image, I decided to shift course. The challenge as I saw it was to identify a *purpose*—one that students would buy into—for understanding how the building blocks of language work together to make meaning.

"I see your point," I said to the students. "Just memorizing parts of speech seems robotic. It gets a lot more interesting, for me anyway, if I think about the *jobs* certain words are doing in a sentence. That feels like a puzzle, and I'm a detective. 'Why do I say things the way I do? How do I know?' Being able to name the kinds of words I use helps me understand better how to use them as a writer."

Suddenly, someone said, "Hey, what part of speech is *because*?"

Another student said, "Yeah! And what about *if*?"

Once again, rescued by student curiosity! We started collecting examples of the words we wanted to learn about, enlisting the help of the school community.

After sorting the input and forming conjectures, we all developed new understandings about phrases and clauses and comma use, not to mention the fact that not all conjunctions are created equal.

For the rest of the year, students paid more attention to how words work together and often asked questions that led to other important inquiries. In fact, we kept a "parking lot" chart to hold questions, which we voted on whenever there was time for further inquiry. During independent project time, individuals or groups might choose one of these to pursue, sharing their results with the class when they were done.

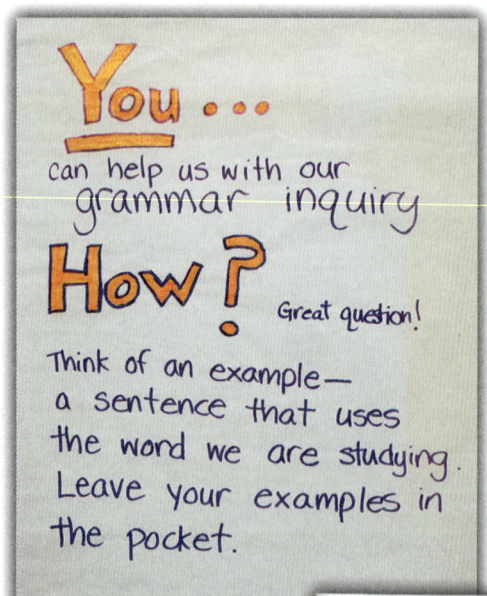

Charts inviting people in the school to help us collect examples of target words for our inquiry

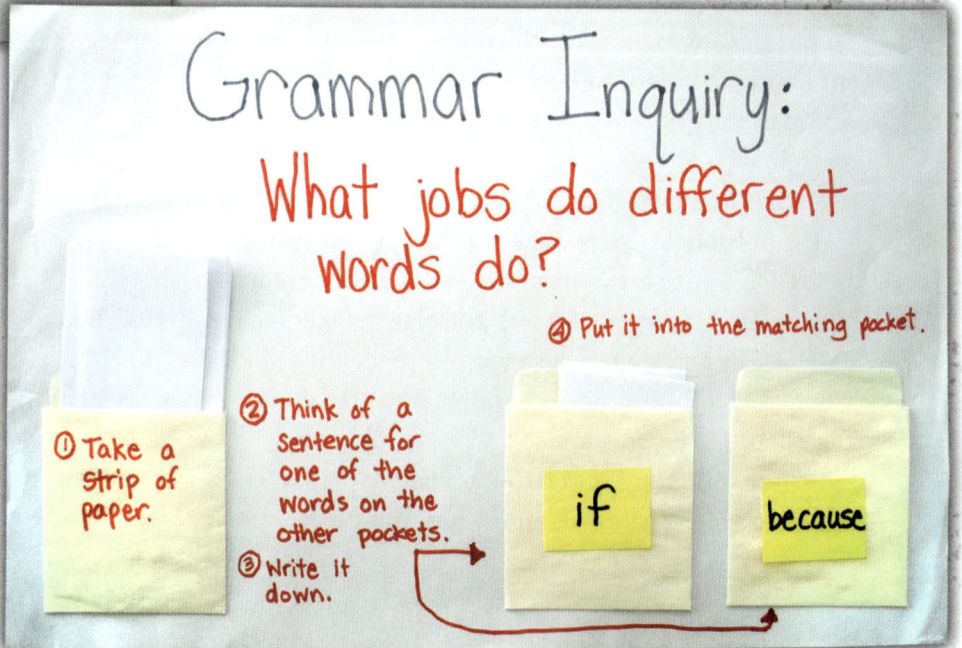

Language Play

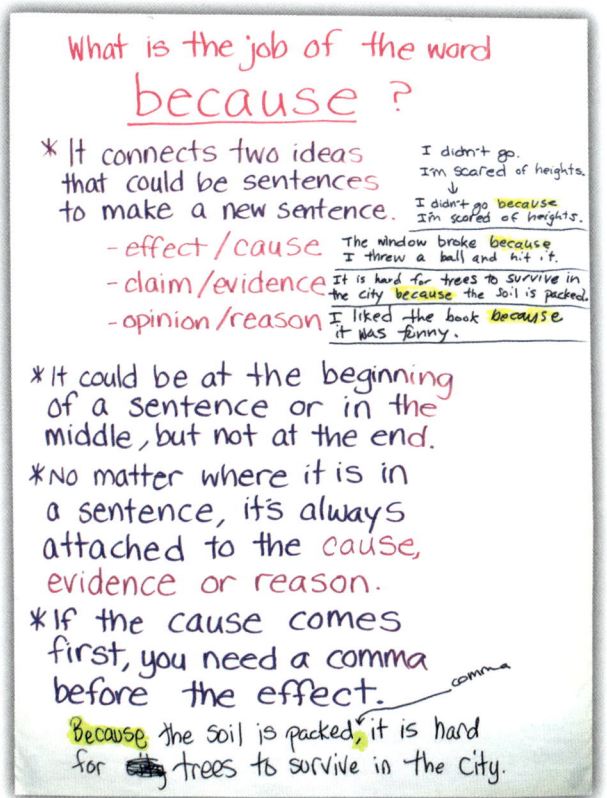
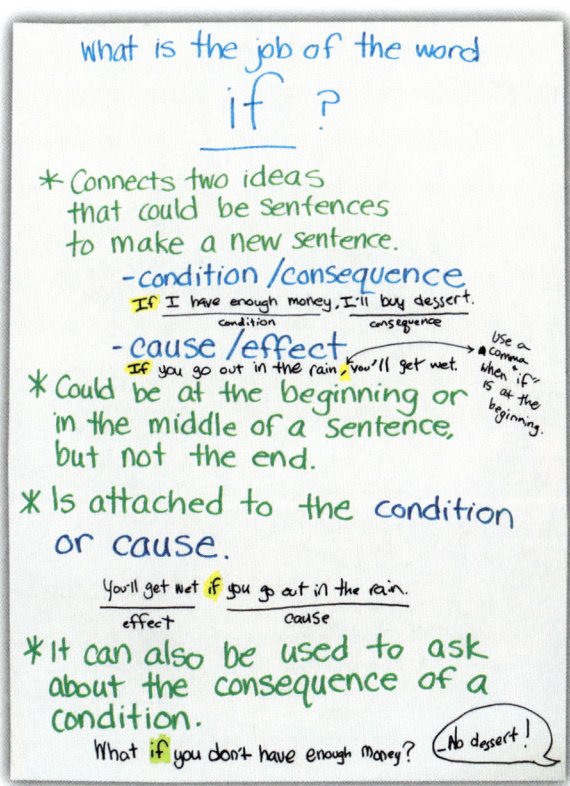

After exploring *because* and *if*, we documented and shared our learning.

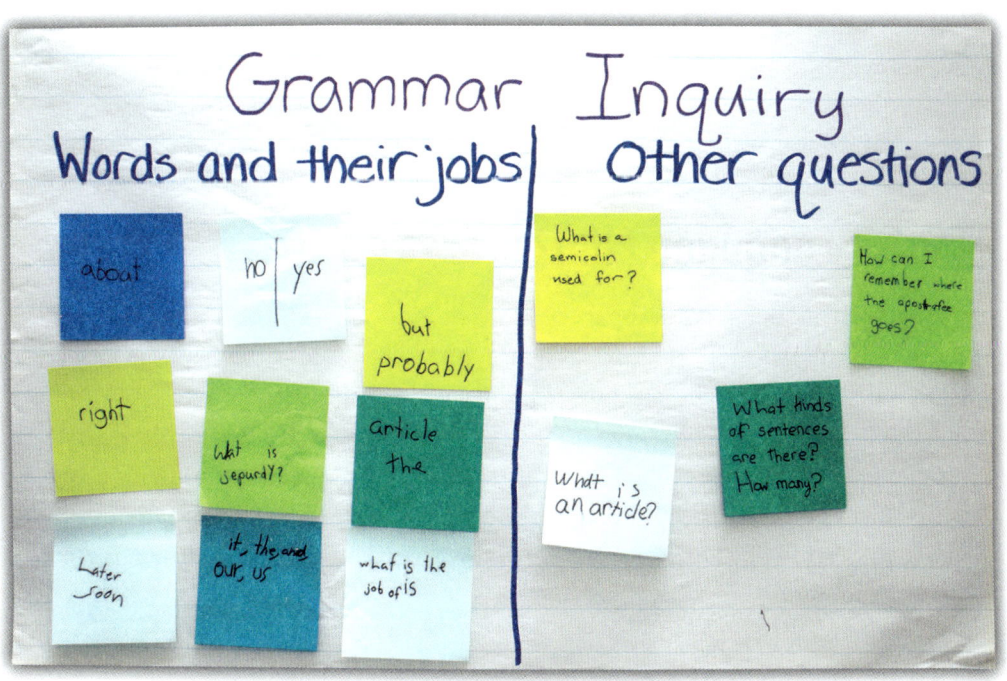

Parking lot chart for collecting students' questions

Play Attention!

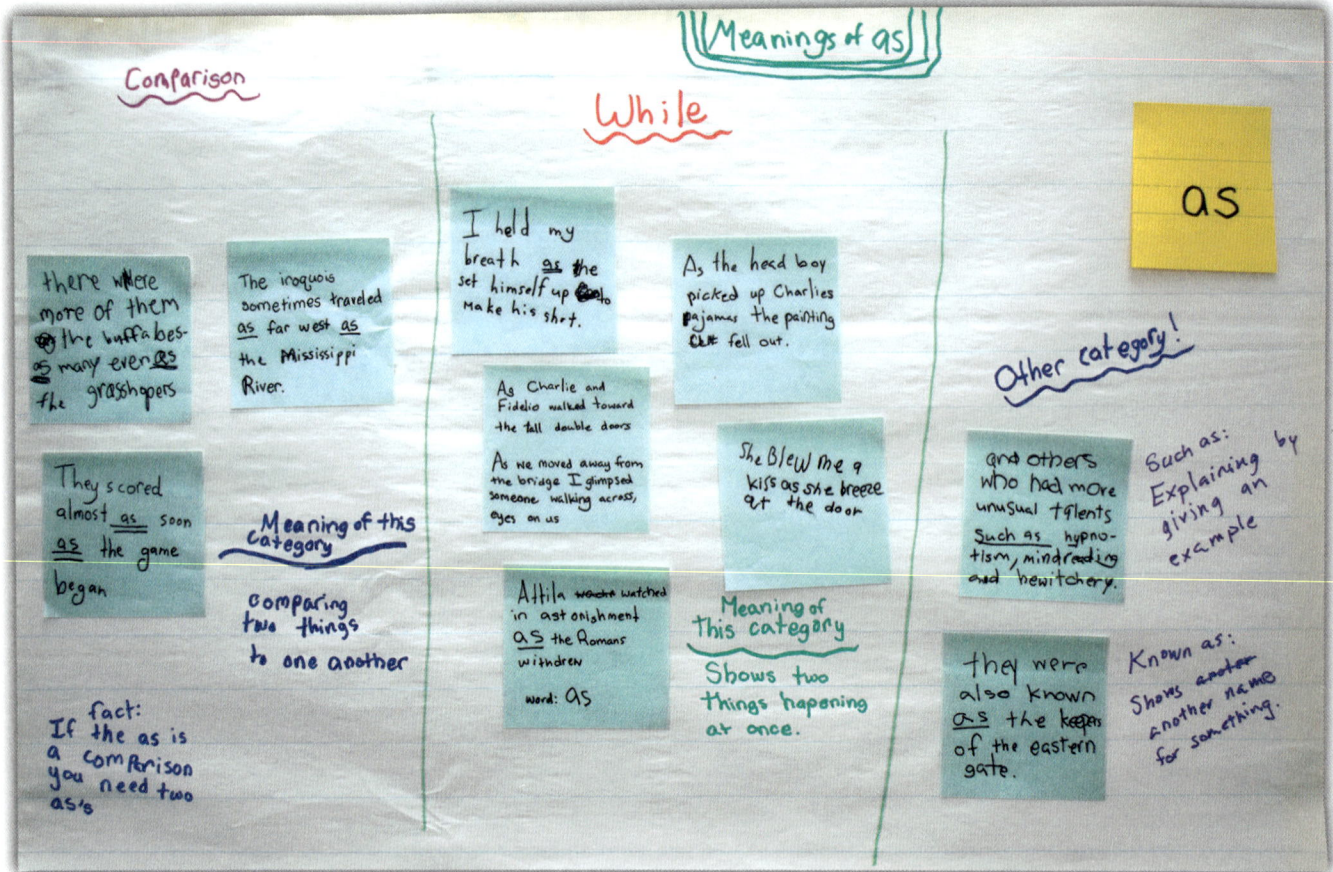

A small group of students documented their exploration of the word *as*. After finding examples in classroom texts, they sorted and categorized them.

These inquiries supported students in meeting standards for language conventions more effectively than any of those swirling worksheets ever could. These examples show how playful inquiry supports meeting New York State Next Generation Standards for English Language Arts.

What Is Language Play?

Language Play is such a natural part of early childhood learning, but the sense of discovery and wonder seems to fade away as kids get older. The worksheets, grammar drills, and vocabulary quizzes replace joy with stress for both students and teachers. These play experiences are meant to bring that spirit back to language learning. They may first be introduced by the teacher, but when they are successful, they often become directed by students. Many of the best playful explorations I've experienced started with offhand comments or questions from students.

> **NEW YORK STATE NEXT GENERATION STANDARDS FOR ENGLISH LANGUAGE ARTS**
>
> **ANCHOR STANDARD L1:** Demonstrate command of the conventions of academic English grammar and usage when writing or speaking.
>
> **Core Conventions Skills for Grades 3 → 5:**
> - Produce simple, compound, and complex sentences.
> - Explain the function of nouns, pronouns, verbs, adjectives, and adverbs in general as well as in particular sentences.
> - Explain the function of conjunctions, prepositions, and interjections in general as well as in particular sentences.
> - Use coordinating and subordinating conjunctions.
>
> **ANCHOR STANDARD L2:** Demonstrate command of the conventions of academic English capitalization, punctuation, and spelling when writing.
>
> **Core Punctuation and Spelling Skills for Grades 3 → 5:**
> - Use a comma before a coordinating conjunction in a compound sentence.

© 2017 NYSED. Used with permission.

Regardless of the aspect of language being explored, Language Play is almost always organized as a whole-class inquiry where we collect information and make sense of it together. Explorations might involve sorting and categorizing words or sentences in an effort to make sense of them. They could involve hunting for and collecting examples of kinds of words or sentences and ordering them in some way, such as intensity of an emotion or complexity of a sentence. Sometimes they start as a game or puzzle I think might spark some interest.

Whatever form it takes, Language Play leads to a deeper understanding of the power of words to change minds, evoke feelings, raise questions, inspire action, or paint vivid images. The aspect of play that seems most evident in Language Play is self-motivation; the students themselves usually come up with an idea of how an exploration should go. Often, small groups or individual students get interested in a question and pursue it on their own during quiet time or as a personal interest project. Language Play is also collaborative and pleasurable, with a greater focus on the process of inquiry than on the final product.

Consider It

Playful exploration with language can support students' learning in three main ways. It can:

- ★ *extend students' vocabulary* in support of reading comprehension and specificity in writing
- ★ engage students in *understanding grammar and structure* in spoken and written language
- ★ strengthen students' *sense and understanding of humor.*

Because some language topics are not immediately interesting to many students, the invitations can be more guided, or the exploration can first be done with the whole class. I don't really need to show students how to play with plastic polygons, for example, but I may need to show them a few ways to play with words before they envision themselves doing so.

Extend Vocabulary

Having a broad vocabulary gives students tools not just to express but also to actually develop increasingly complex ideas. Yet it's not easy to find authentic and engaging ways to build vocabulary, nor is there an abundance of time to implement a comprehensive program. Playful explorations are relatively quick, require little planning, and can become a monthly (or less frequent) routine. The explorations in this category focus on words in two main ways: playing with roots and affixes while learning about their origins and collecting sets of words with similar meanings while teasing out their nuances.

Language Play to explore word meanings by tracing their origins might not always start with students' curiosity but can quickly lead to it. The first time I engaged with a class in an exploration, it started with me showing students something *I* thought was fun. I didn't dream it would become a playful experience, but modeling my own curiosity and interest acted as an unintentional invitation. When I saw students take an interest, I became more deliberate in planning explorations of word parts. A few times throughout the school year, I incorporate a brief lesson or exploration about a word that's important in a current unit of study, such as *community* or *revolution*. I look up its etymology and find a way to present it that makes sense to students, usually with a web or chart that shows connections to other words.

Vocabulary explorations can also focus on meaning and tone, rather than origin. By collecting, sorting, and categorizing words that have similar meanings,

> **The explorations in this category are especially helpful for students learning English and can easily be adapted to use in small groups.**

we enable students to communicate their ideas more precisely in speech and in writing. A concrete way to organize this is by degree of intensity. Students can begin by learning a range of words between *pleased* and *ecstatic*, for example. Students who already have fairly sophisticated vocabularies will be ready to explore different kinds of nuances, such as the difference between *ask* and *inquire*, *home* and *dwelling*, or *tasty* and *delicious*.

Understand Grammar and Structure

All languages and dialects have their underlying structures, the written and unwritten formulas we follow when speaking or writing, and most of us have an internalized dialect, the product of our upbringing and environment. The degree to which our dialects resemble the "academic English" presumed in language standards varies widely. Nonetheless, we all follow some kind of consistent set of rules for language use. An important goal of these explorations is to increase students' awareness of and interest in the structures and guiding principles that inform how we communicate. In the process of working toward this goal, students also gain more concrete knowledge of academic English. Explorations of grammar and structure can look at parts of speech, punctuation, or kinds of sentences—basically any aspect of usage you want students to explore.

Webs help students visualize connections among words.

Make Sense of and Understand Humor

A well-developed sense of humor is important not only for emotional well-being but also for cognitive flexibility, creative problem-solving, and comprehension of spoken and written text that is not straightforward. Researchers have shown that in elementary school students, a sense of humor correlates highly with both intelligence and creativity, but that the correlation between intelligence and creativity is very low (Hauck and Thomas 1972). In other words, children with a sense of humor, regardless of how they perform on an IQ test, are more likely to be creative.

In a version of Karl Duncker's (1945) famous "Candle Problem," groups of college students were given a box of thumbtacks, a candle, and some matches and asked to attach the candle to the wall in such a way that it would not drip wax onto the table or floor. The students who watched five minutes of comedy before being given the task were more likely to solve it than those who watched a negative or neutral film clip, those who watched no film clip, and even those who were given a candy bar (Isen, Daubman, and Nowicki 1987). Humor makes us better at figuring stuff out!

We all know the expressions *wordplay* or a *play on words*, and that's what we explore in these playful experiences. What makes a pun funny or a double entendre mysterious? How does word choice help you land the perfect joke? Was that malaprop intentional?! There are so many possibilities, and these explorations help students understand the wonderful, nimble way language *itself* is play.

Imagine It

More than in other chapters, the examples I've included to help you imagine Language Play may seem to fall into one category more than the others. Nevertheless, the purposes and learning outcomes still overlap, creating ample opportunity for an exploration into word origins to lead into one about parts of speech, for instance. In each example, I will highlight particular words that made sense for my students and purposes at the time, but each kind of exploration is adaptable to *any* language content you wish to explore.

Breaking Words Together

By turning their attention to the histories and meanings of common roots and prefixes, students not only learn new words but also acquire tools to approximate the meanings of unfamiliar words. If you plant the seed early in the year as you and your class are getting to know each other, you can start by exploring the etymology of a relevant word, such as *community*, *educate*, or *respect*. With the whole class, show students how roots and prefixes have historical meanings that contribute to our modern definitions of words, then chart this work so that students can see connections among words.

It's helpful to talk students through the different parts of a word, thinking aloud about how they work together to make the meaning we now associate with the word. For example, for the word *community*, I might explain:

Com- is kind of like co- *or* con-. *It means "with" or "together." Like co-teachers are teachers who work together.* Muni *comes from the Latin word for "duties" or "jobs." It actually even goes back further than that to a word that means trading or exchanging things. That makes me think about the idea that people don't have everything they need, but if they trade some of what they have, everyone can have what they need. The* -ity *at the end shows that it's a noun. So all together, we can think of a* community *as a group of people who are doing their jobs together so that everyone's needs are met.*

As you explain words like this over time (it's more likely to capture students' imaginations if not too much time passes between exposures), students start to see relationships and notice other words they know with a root or prefix in common with a word on the chart. They also often begin to guess at meanings. In fact, breaking words becomes a habit of mind you can use when you explore words in other contexts. For example, in one class, an exploration of homophones (described later in this chapter) led us back to breaking words when we looked at *homo-* and *-phone*.

An exploration of homophones led to a session of breaking words together.

Here's bit of the conversation that happened with the homophone chart:

Theo: Well, I know *homo-* means "same" and *-phone* means "sound," so they're words that sound the same.

Me: [*Writing the meanings under the word parts*] Yeah, so here's another word with *-phone: telephone.*

Anna: What's *tele-*?

Bryce: Is it "machine" or something like that?

Me: *Tele-* is "far."

Cady: Ooh, like hearing someone who's far away.

Me: Interesting right? Are there other *tele-* words you can think of?

DaShawn: *Teleport*!

Evan: Then what's *port*?

Cady: It must be like "travel."

Gaby: Or "move."

Theo: Yeah, because *portable*.

Me: We could keep making connections for hours! I'm going to leave this chart up so you can add ideas and questions whenever they come to you. Theo, write down *portable* here and we'll keep looking at *port* next time.

One Part, Many Words

This playful exploration is really just a student-led version of breaking words together. With some experience, children will start to notice word parts everywhere they look, coming up with their own ideas about how to explore words and document their learning. You might make this a predictable structure every week or two for fifteen to twenty minutes, as either a student-directed whole-class inquiry or small-group self-directed projects.

There are several ways these playful explorations can go. Students might explore one root with many connected words, as in *transmit, submit, omit, emit,* and so on, or one prefix attached to many roots, as in *submerge, submarine, subordinate, submit,* and *substitute.* You can support this by thinking aloud about words you find puzzling or interesting ("*Construction* and *destruction* are such similar words but they mean almost the opposite of each other! I wonder what that's about . . .").

Show students how they can google a word plus "etymology" to find out more, or go to the website, etymonline.com, to find the origins of words. Other websites, such as Reading Rockets and Wikipedia, offer lists of roots and their meanings, with sample words, enabling students to look up roots and not just whole words. Children doing this work in partnerships or small groups will generate their own ways of documenting and sharing their findings.

---

*I know that **port** does not mean "travel" or "move," so why not just say this? Well, I decided against it because the time I've allotted for this conversation is almost up; we could go on forever if it weren't for the timer. More importantly, Evan has just provided the perfect opportunity to put students in the driver's seat of this work.*

Language Play

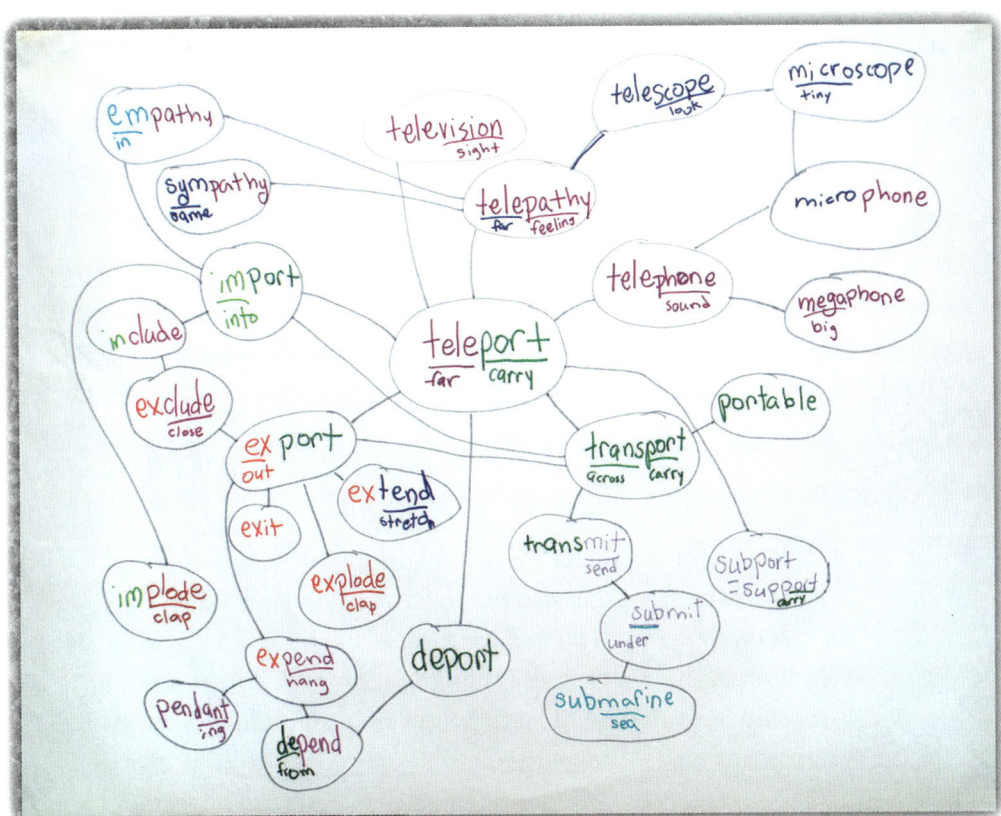

A group of fifth graders built this web of words over a few sessions.

A group of fourth-grade friends created this pocket chart.

A note on the power and gratification of doing this from time to time: In the spring, when I put up the word constitution, *my students knew that* con- *means "with" and* stit *means "stand," so they were able to discuss the Constitution as a document that represented people standing together. Wow.*

Word Endings

If you are breaking a lot of words together, there is a good chance that at some point students will notice and wonder about the endings of words. You can capitalize on their curiosity by showing them how, unlike prefixes, suffixes often denote a word's part of speech, rather than affecting its meaning. Exposure to different forms of a word, such as *express*, *expression*, and *expressive*, helps students understand how to identify and use words as different parts of speech. This can become a language study inquiry the whole class digs into for a few brief sessions, or some students may decide to take it on in independent project time.

An exploration of word endings usually sounds something like this conversation my students and I had about the word *attention*:

> **Me:** This was surprising for me. I thought the *ten* in *attention* came from a different root that means "to have or hold onto something." But it actually is from *tend*, which means "to stretch." So, paying attention is more active than I thought. It's more effort to stretch your mind to something than to simply hold something. I guess that explains why it can be hard!
>
> **Anton:** Like *ex*tend is to stretch further or bigger.
>
> **Me:** [*Adding* extend *to the chart*] Yeah, the *ex-* is "out" or "outward," like *exit*. And the *at-* at the beginning means "toward." Stretching toward.
>
> **Bryce:** So then, is *in*tend "to stretch inward"?
>
> **Me:** Hmm. Let's see. [*Looking it up*] The *in-* for *intend* is also "toward." So, they're saying it's like stretching toward a plan or a purpose if you intend to do something.
>
> **Celeste:** Why does *in-* mean so many things?
>
> **Me:** I know, right? Put that on the parking lot. I have no idea!
>
> **Damian:** What is *-tion*?
>
> **Me:** Um . . .
>
> **Eli:** It's not making a whole different word, like *extend* or *intend* . . .
>
> **Damian:** It's making a verb into a noun! It's a nounerizer.

If amazing questions like "What is *-tion*?" come up while you are focused on another word, simply ask students to add it to the parking lot. This will give you time to craft it into an invitation for a whole-class or small-group inquiry like this:

> *Remember last week when we were looking at the word* attention *and Damian said that –*tion *is a nounerizer? I've been thinking about that. Eli said it doesn't change the meaning, like* in- *or* ex-, *and Damian said it makes the word a noun. So, my question for you is, are there other –izers? How can we find out?*

To get an exploration rolling, you might brainstorm some examples together as a class. I started off with *attention* and *attentive*, referring to the word that got us into this question in the first place. Endings that are likely to come up include *-ing, -ly, -al, -ism, -ist, -er, -ed, -ist, -ic*, and also combinations of these, such as *-ally, -istic,* and *-istically*. Someone might even suggest *-esque*! Then, to continue the exploration, students might:

★ look at charts in the room for similar words with different endings

★ use a dictionary (or online dictionary) to find versions of a word

★ brainstorm words that can have different endings.

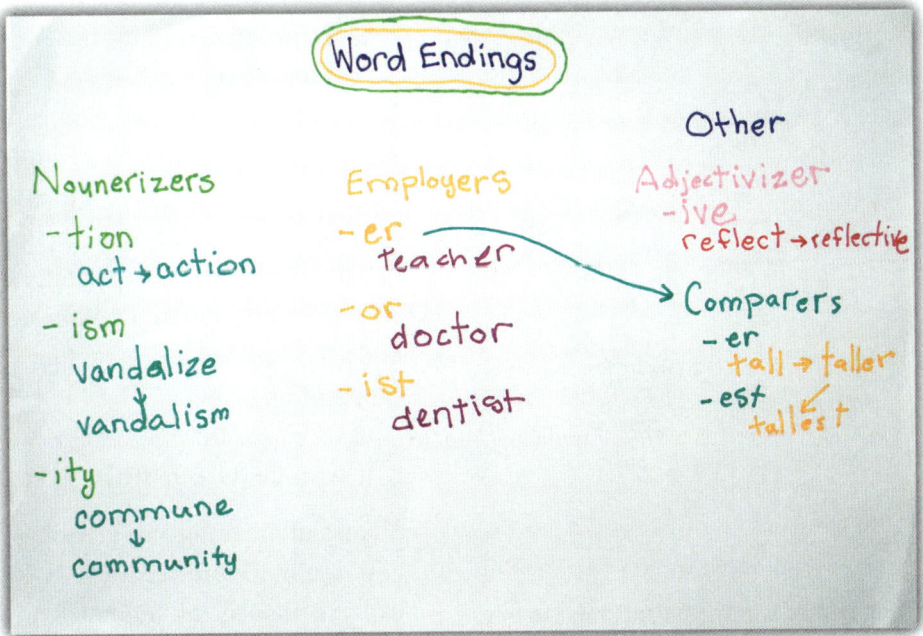

A group of fourth graders documenting their inquiry into word endings

Word Relatives

Collecting and exploring words with similar domains or meanings helps students build their vocabulary, giving them more precise ways to express themselves when speaking and writing. For example, *kind*, *caring*, *generous*, *friendly*, and *welcoming* are all more precise alternatives to *nice*.

With the whole class, gather sets of words most students are familiar with. I find it helpful to start with emotions, since all children have them and can come up with a few ways to express them. An early set of word relatives might include *happy*, *glad*, *delighted*, and *excited*, for example. Then, as you encounter new words in a read-aloud or a unit of study, or as students come across them in their independent work, add them to an existing collection or start a new one: "Oh, an aroma is a scent or a smell. We can start a *smell* bubble."

For students to use and update the word collections independently, be sure to organize them graphically in a way that is consistent and makes sense to you and your students. For example, it may make more sense to group related words in big "blobs," or in rows, columns, or boxes. Then, as a whole class, revisit your collections periodically to talk about the updates and see what new thinking they might offer.

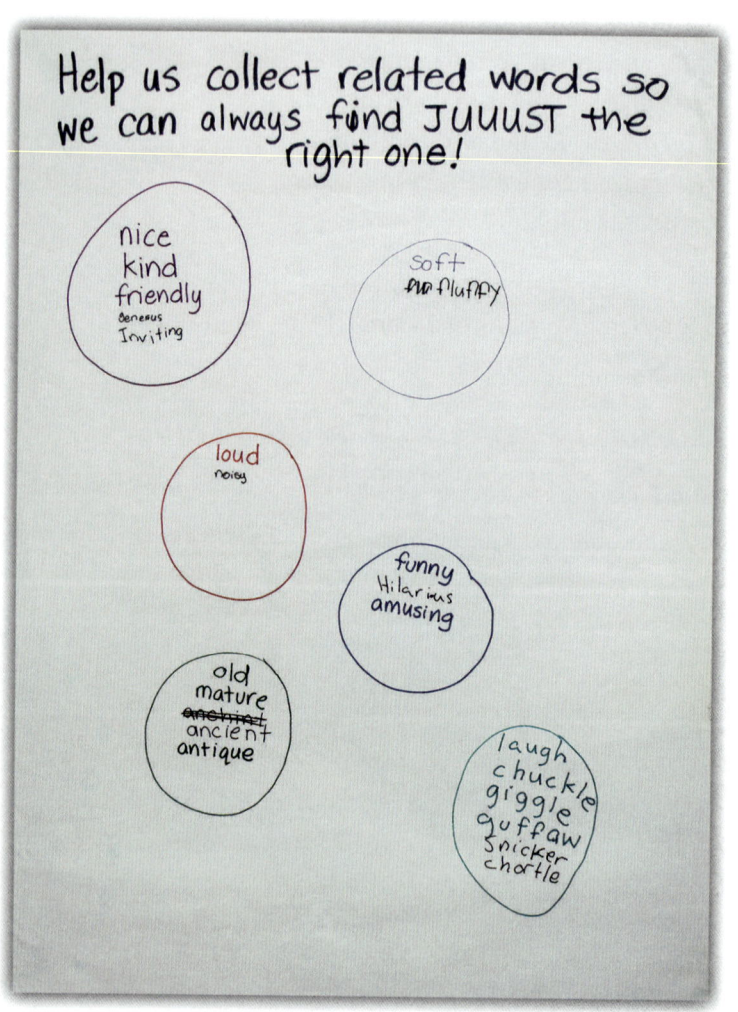

A third-grade class is collecting related words. Students refer to this chart when writing.

Shades of Meaning

Shades of meaning also gives children more precise ways to express themselves, but here the focus is on collecting related words that differ in the degree of intensity. If you have collections of word relatives, you can use some of those groups to start exploring more subtle shades of meaning.

Start by showing students how you can put a set of words in order from least to most intense. Think aloud about each word, how you use it, and how it compares to the others in the group.

> *Disgusting* is more disgusting than just *gross, but not as disgusting as* repulsive, *I think.*

You can represent this thinking in several ways. You might jot numbers next to the words on a chart (if you have one already from collecting word relatives), write them in order onto a new organizer, or have the words you are exploring all written on strips of paper that you move around as you decide the order. After you've sorted words by intensity as a whole class, you might give small groups of students other sets of words to discuss and arrange.

Expert Words

Students also benefit from gathering academic, domain-specific vocabulary related to the content they are studying. Of course, content area word walls have been around a long time, but when you put the creation and presentation of them into students' hands, the whole process becomes more playful and students are more likely to remember the words they're collecting. Also, as they learn about new content, students often get invested in thinking about ways to teach it to others, which is a perfect hook for collecting expert words.

Consider developing a space and a routine for keeping track of important new words as they come up during a content area study. For example, when

Paint chips are a useful tool for arranging words in order of intensity. This class has a basket of blank chips available for students to use for projects.

These strips are laminated so that students can use dry-erase markers on them, enabling them to change words as needed.

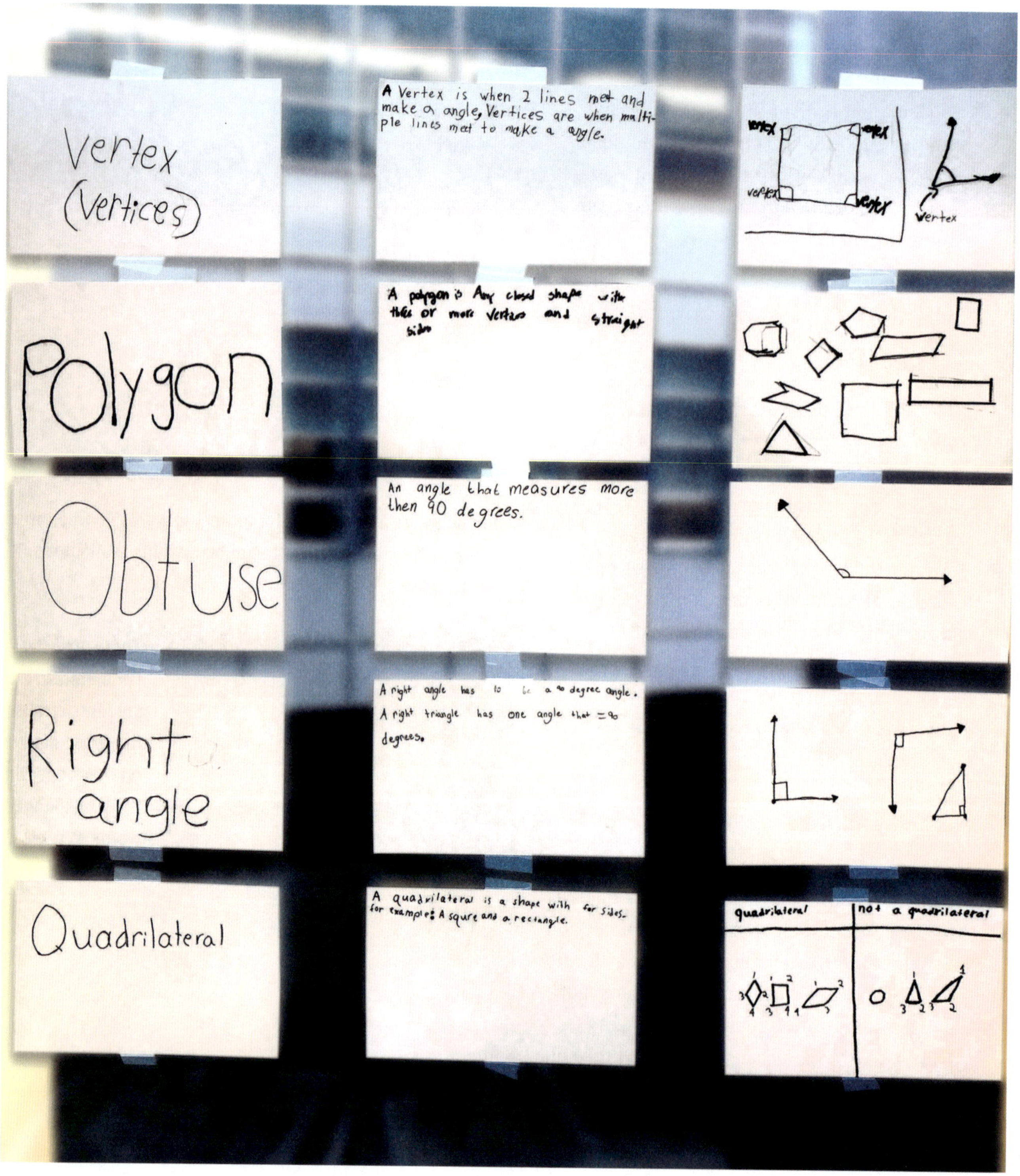

Geometry word definitions created by fourth graders

you encounter new vocabulary in a lesson, an exploration, or a read-aloud, you might take a few minutes and ask students how they would explain or illustrate the word in kid language. Then have a couple of students create a definition with an illustration or example to go on a chart. Because the charted collection of words is cumulative, it can be used as a reference. This works well in subjects like math where students need to know the vocabulary (*factor* and *multiple*, for example) as they do the work.

Another approach is to keep a running list of words (*wigwam*, *longhouse*, *three sisters garden*, etc.) and devote a period or two to writing "kid language" definitions and making or finding illustrations. In this case, the illustrated chart is an artifact of learning that happened during the unit rather than a reference. During a final celebration, the expert word wall becomes an exhibit and students might act as docents for family and friends.

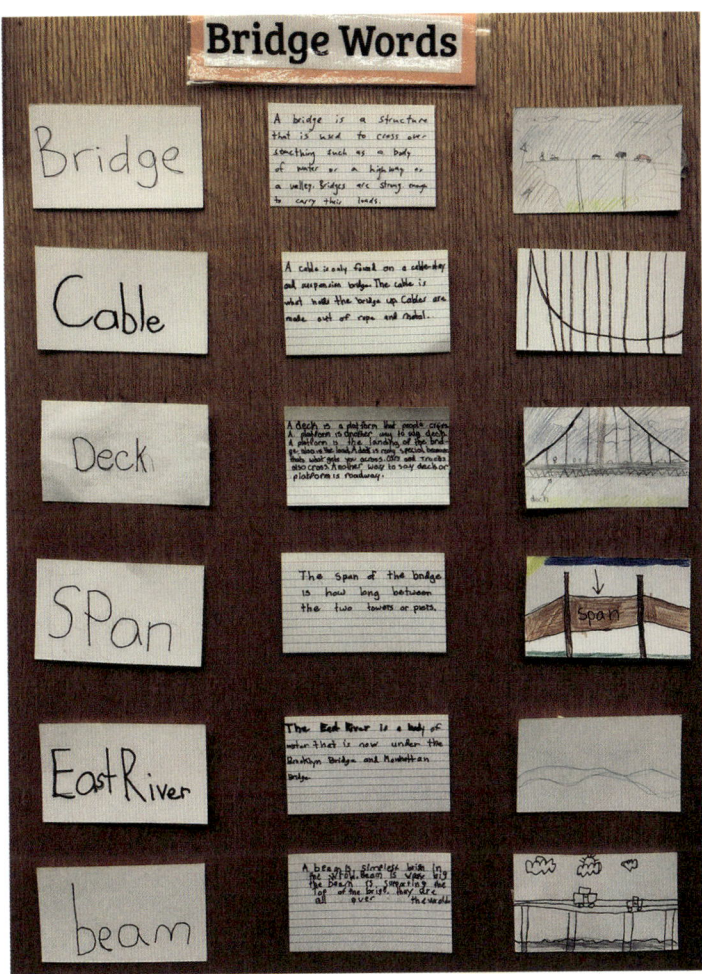

Third graders made a visual word wall as they learned vocabulary related to their study of bridges.

Word Textures

Besides having a vocabulary for expressing ideas on a more granular level, writers also consider how words sound in the ear or feel in the mouth. For example, consider the following two descriptions of going up stairs:

> My sneakers slapped each step as I raced upward.

> The smooth soles of my shoes seemed to melt onto each stair as I climbed upward.

Notice that it's not just the meanings of the words but also their sounds that contribute to the contrasting images of movement. Awareness of the power of words, even at the level of sound, gives students tools for both reading and writing texts.

This exploration into the sounds of words is adapted from a poetry center I first heard about from Georgia Heard (1999). It is particularly well suited to support reading and writing poetry, though you will find strong examples in all kinds of prose (especially in picture books). The invitation can be embedded in a read-aloud, focusing students' attention on how certain words sound in their ears or feel in their mouths as they repeat them, and how that can affect meaning.

For example, the picture book *Stick and Stone* (2015) by Beth Ferry (illustrated by Tom Lichtenheld) is a sensual sound experience, beginning with the contrast between the sound of the two main characters' names. With a book like this, I would have students say each name several times—*Stick, Stone*—and really listen to how different they sound, notice the different ways the mouth moves to say each one, and think about how different they "feel" to the ear. Then I would model my thinking about the sounds:

> The o and the n in Stone are just so much softer when I say them, almost gooey in my mouth. The sound of Stick is so much sharper. Stick. Hmm, I wonder if those contrasts will be meaningful as we read this book. Let's listen for them and for others.

And in this particular book, students will hear many interesting, contrasting words such as *thunder and rain*, *pinecone*, *windblown*, and *muddle*. The key is to get students paying attention to how words sound (in addition to what they mean).

Students can then explore texts in partnerships, collecting and sorting words with interesting textures. Providing preselected texts, such as a packet of poems, and a few suggested textures, such as smooth, sharp, bumpy, and gooey, will give students more support. Once students' attention is drawn to the idea that the sound and texture of words matters, they will discover a lot in a single period. If you have them designate a few pages of their word study or writing notebooks to collecting words with different textures, it will help them maintain this awareness and they can continue to explore the "mouthfeel" or "earfeel" of words on their own. You can also make this exploration a literacy center.

Word Instructions

To me, being able to identify parts of speech seems a lot like being able to recite times tables—evidence of memorization that doesn't reveal anything about understanding. This playful exploration shifts the focus from identification

Language Play   87

Word Textures:

As you notice the textures of words that you hear or read, collect them here.

Smooth	Bumpy	Sharp	Gooey
River	Hippopotamus	Crack	Ground
wish	racket	krocket	jooey
feather	rambunchious	cough	sludge
knife	brick	cricket	bubble
piano	tredmill		grass

Now that you've collected some words, what do you notice about any of these categories?

some letters sound smoother than others like sh sounds smoother than ck

Word Textures:

As you notice the textures of words that you hear or read, collect them here.

Smooth	Bumpy	Sharp	Gooey
River	Hippopotamus	Crack	Ground

Now that you've collected some words, what do you notice about any of these categories?

Students can collect words as they come up in their reading, using a sheet taped into their notebooks.

> Sometimes words sound like what they mean. I was just thinking about rambunctious. Rambunctious. Ram is kind of smooth and then BUNC comes along and feels kind of bouncy. Then tious sort of slips away. Slow is slow and fast is fast. My mom hates the word moist. When she said that I said moist moist moist moist moist moist... Then I felt like my mouth was doing a fish mouth thing. It was kind of gross but I didn't want my mom to know I thought it was gross but she could tell and she said see?

This student was inspired to write a whole entry in his notebook about the word *rambunctious*.

to understanding by challenging students to define the *job* a word is doing in a sentence. Through inquiry and inductive reasoning, students discover many "rules" of the language. You need only two or three class periods, preferably no more than a week apart, to explore and develop conjectures about the function of a particular word or set of words.

Before the exploration, prepare cards or slips of paper with the words you want to explore written on them. Your invitation can simply be a question, as when Daniela asked, "What's the difference between *who* and *whom*?" or it may be a broader invitation, "Let's figure out what work these words do." In some cases it helps to briefly demonstrate how to approach defining the jobs of the words:

> *If I use the words in sentences, it will help me figure out how they're different. Let's see . . . "I am a* careful *driver. I drive* carefully*." I can't say, "I'm a* carefully *driver."*

Give sets of words to small groups and have them work together to write instructions for using them. As they come up with ideas, examples, and conjectures, give out larger paper and glue sticks so they can document their process. The example shows third graders working together to figure out how adjectives and adverbs are used differently. They guess that both words are adjectives because both words are describing. In the next session, I will give them the academic vocabulary of *adjective* and *adverb*.

A word instruction exploration can focus on language usage in lots of ways, such as:

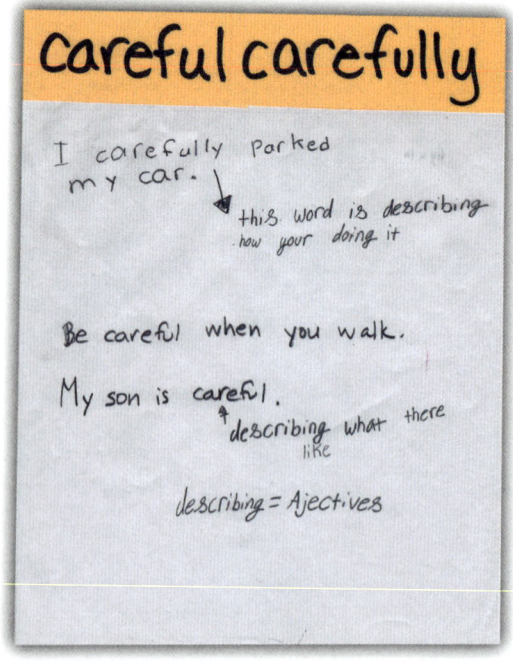

Third graders exploring the jobs that adjectives and adverbs do

★ pronouns

★ verb tenses

★ subject-verb agreement (*I, you, he/she, they, we,* paired with a variety of verbs)

★ kinds of plural nouns (brainstorm a list of nouns, making sure to include things that result in plurals that don't simply have an *s* on the end (e.g., *sheep, fish, child, man/woman, person,* then also words where the singular ends in *s*)

★ prepositions.

Language Play   89

I	**me**	**my**	**mine**	**myself**	Refering to yourself
you	you	your	yours	yourself	Referring to someone you're talking to
you	You	your	your's	yourselves	Referring to a group of people you're not in, when talking to them.
he	him	his	his	himself	Referring to a male
she	her	her	hers	Herself	Referring to a female
they	them	their	theirs	themselves	Referring to a group of people * Also can be used as a nonbinary pronoun (themself for one person)
We	Us	Our	Ours	Ourselves	
These people are doing an action	someone else is doing an action to these people	Possesive followed by a word	Possesive sentence ender Or used before a comma	When the person doing the action is the same as the person it's being done to.	

One group's pronoun grid with student-generated descriptions of categories that match case, person, gender, and number. All groups in the class started with *I*, *me*, *my*, *mine*, and *myself* and approached the question differently.

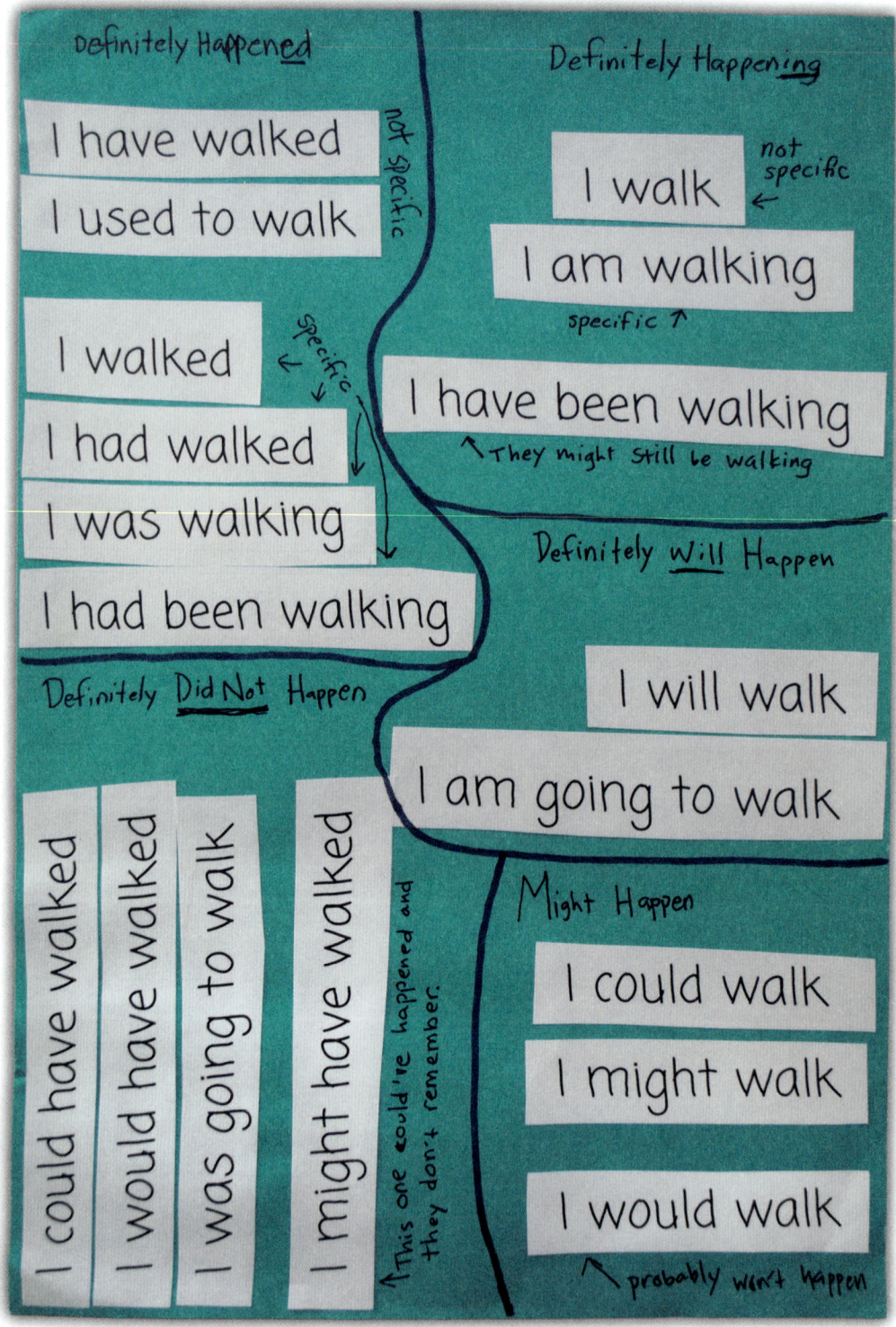

This sixth grader's exploration of verb tenses proved to be a support for him in his French class.

Puns and Homophones

When I think about the homophones we most want students to be aware of, the most commonly confused sound-alike words *their*, *there*, and *they're* come to mind first. But in creating this exploration, I wanted to draw students' attention to a broader range of words that sound the same but have different spellings.

A single class period is enough time for students to play with pairs of words in fun ways. In two periods, students can hone the humor of their word pairs and create more detailed pictures or comics to illustrate their scenarios. The invitation for this exploration needs to include examples. There are many books of illustrated puns and homophones to inspire students to create humorous misuses of words. I like to read aloud a book I had loved in my own childhood, *The King Who Rained* (1999), by Fred Gwynne. I also show students an example I made myself after dreaming about it one night (see below).

After showing students a few examples and reviewing or explaining what homophones are, brainstorm a list of words that sound alike but are spelled differently. It's helpful to gather several pairs of words ahead of time in case

My example of homophone play

Students helped brainstorm a list of homophones to play with.

students have trouble getting started with a list. They can work in pairs or small groups to create scenarios with comics or drawings.

Fifth graders play with words.

This sixth grader uses French words to make puns in comics.

Plan It

For Language Play to be successful, it's important to have a strong invitation, thoughtfully prepared materials, and some sense of learning targets so that your feedback is both lean and effective. To begin your planning, identify a primary purpose by thinking about something you want to teach in a new way or a problem of practice. This might be something you observe in students, curriculum, or your own past teaching. For example:

- ★ My students need to be able to identify and use adjectives and adverbs properly. Direct teaching and worksheets haven't been engaging for them, and the learning hasn't transferred into their own writing.

- ★ I want to teach vocabulary in a way that students are actually invested in, so they'll have the tools to learn new words independently.

- ★ If one more person says, "Me and my friend went to the park," I'm going to cry.

Approaching language systems as inquiry, rather than direct teaching, is a great way to make it feel more playful. This means creating a sense of adventure, infusing the explorations with the spirit of "this could go absolutely anywhere!" For example, when you invite students to play, try casting them as detectives with a mystery to solve or scientists with a question to answer.

> I, me, myself—Why do we need so many words for the same person? What are all the number word beginnings, like uni-, bi-, and tri-? Is there one for every number? Like twenty-three?

Students can then work in small groups to gather examples and draw conclusions, or they might sort and categorize information and create criteria for the categories.

If students have language study notebooks, they can record much of their thinking about Language Play there. Just remember, explorations feel more playful when students can manipulate materials first to try out ideas—sorting words in different ways and moving them around to make their thinking visible. For example, grouping all the words that start with *con-* sparks different thinking that grouping all the words with *junc* in them. Luckily, the materials for Language Play are fairly simple. It's helpful to have:

- ★ large construction paper
- ★ colored paper or cardstock (for cutting strips and cards)

- ★ scissors
- ★ glue sticks
- ★ markers or Sharpies.

For explorations requiring research, such as those involving Greek or Latin origins or finding examples of certain kinds of words, students will need resources to find information:

- ★ selected mentor texts
- ★ laptops or tablets
- ★ dictionaries
- ★ thesauri
- ★ grammar or style guides.

If you play with the materials you've selected for the exploration first yourself, you'll gain insight that can guide how you roll out the exploration with students. Consider questions such as:

- ★ Do I need to adjust the materials? For example, would it work better for small groups to have their words in different-color strips?
- ★ How much time will students need to explore? One period, several in a row, several over time . . . ?
- ★ Will the exploration be more open-ended, or should there be a project in mind? (A project could still be open-ended, given students will find their own way to do it.)
- ★ What kinds of things are children likely to do with the materials and the topic?
- ★ Where might students go with this? What discoveries might they make? What misconceptions could emerge?
- ★ What questions/feedback can I offer to support their learning?

Language Play

The Framework in Action for Language Play

INVITE

Invitations for Language Play should spark curiosity, and they can come from the teacher or from students. I find it helpful to approach a topic as a kind of puzzle. When I show children how I playfully explore a language puzzle (actual fun, not fake fun), they usually want to chime in or ask for similar puzzles to explore.

★ *Isn't it weird how so many words related to teeth have* dent *or* dont *in them?*

★ *Sometimes I notice a few words that have a part in common, and I wonder if they're actually related or if it's a coincidence.*

★ *Sometimes I'm reading your notebooks and I see sentences like, "It was really, really old," or "I was so so so so so excited!" I'm thinking we could find words to say what we want to say without using* really *or* so.

★ *I know it's so confusing when you're supposed to use* I *and when* me *is the correct word. Maybe we can figure it out by looking at times when we know for sure that each one is the better choice.*

When invitations come from students, you'll need to decide whether it makes sense to extend it to the whole class or whether it should be an independent or small-group exploration. Either way, you can work with students to determine the form their inquiry will take and what materials will be helpful.

Here, for example, are two student questions that started inquiries in my classroom:

How come "five" is sometimes *penta-* and sometimes *quint-*?

Why does *in* at the beginning of a word sometimes mean "in" and sometimes mean "not"?

(continues)

The Framework in Action for Language Play *(continued)*

PLAY

Observe

Listening is very important as you observe children engaged in Language Play, but you'll also want to look closely at what students do to support their thinking and watch how they use the resources or materials. Ask yourself questions like these:

★ *Is anyone forming conjectures or making generalizations? If so, how are they getting there?*

★ *Are they talking about what they find out? How?*

★ *Do you see evidence of misconceptions? Is the conversation resolving them, or might you need to offer some clarity?*

★ *What kind of information are they looking for? Examples? Definitions? Categories?*

★ *Are they organizing their findings? How?*

★ *Do they stick with one idea or follow several different paths?*

★ *Are they working with a single variable or more (i.e., one part of speech, root or affix, method)?*

★ *Do you see students working separately with a similar idea? Would a discussion or collaboration benefit them?*

★ *Do students know how to use the resources that are part of this exploration?*

As with most kinds of play, photos can be a particularly useful form of documentation if students aren't documenting their processes themselves.

Provide Lean Input

Offer questions or thoughts that further students in their own lines of inquiry or scaffold a discovery they're on the verge of making. As they explore, ask questions such as:

★ *Have you seen or heard this somewhere before?*

★ *How will you explore this?*

★ *How did you decide on these categories? How do you know these go together?*

★ *What do you notice about how _____ (words, word parts, phrases, etc.) work together?*

★ *Do you want to work with someone else who's exploring a similar question?*

★ *Is there a pattern? Does the pattern exist with different words, roots, affixes, tenses, etc?*

★ *Is this always true? When is or isn't it?*

★ *How could you document this for future reference or to share with the class?*

Keep an eye out for students who may benefit from having another resource or material to support their exploration or documentation of learning.

The Framework in Action for Language Play *(continued)*

REFLECT

Whether you reflect purely in conversation or also in writing, some possible questions to include are:

★ What was fun? Interesting? Surprising?

★ What was challenging?

★ What did you find out?

★ How did this affect your understanding of language?

★ Are you thinking of doing a similar exploration?

If individuals, partnerships, or groups have created documents of their learning, you might consider having them do a gallery walk and comment on one another's notes and discoveries. You might also ask questions like these to consider how you can document learning for the whole class:

★ Did anyone else's work give you new ideas about your own?

★ Do you have new questions?

★ What would make this work better next time?

If any charts or documents seem to be a useful reference, either type them up or print photographs of them to tape into students' notebooks.

CHAPTER FIVE

COLLABORATION PLAY

To the art of working well a civilized [people] would add the art of playing well.
—George Santayana, American philosopher

Like most teachers, I always involved my students in the coauthoring of norms for our classroom community at the start of each new year. A conversation with one class opened my eyes to the need to do this in a more substantive way—a way that invited students not only to draft agreements as a class but also to envision the rights they felt they should have as learners and the responsibilities they saw attached to those rights.

One day while talking about the U.S. Constitution with my fourth-grade class, an interesting question came up: How is it possible that American children are not guaranteed a free education? All of us, including me, thought that a free, public education was a federal Constitutional right. It's not. (Oddly, it *is* a right to have an *equal* education in states whose own constitutions guarantee a free public education, but that's not part of this story.) Being in New York, we quickly looked up what our own state guarantees, which is a "sound, basic education."

Someone said, sarcastically, "Well, *that's* helpful!"

Sensing an opportunity, I asked, "What would be more helpful? What do you think your rights as learners should be?"

I can't tell you how anyone responded because they all started talking at once! Clearly the question struck a nerve and needed to be addressed. Just not right then in the last ten minutes before lunch. I asked students to write their thoughts on slips of paper, feeling free to talk to one another about it if they wanted to. As I read their words, I wondered why I had never thought to ask this question before. Perhaps I had worried they'd ask for candy and all-day recess. As usual, they exceeded my expectations. Here are a few of their responses:

- ★ to have fun learning as long as it doesn't disturb anyone
- ★ to not be teased when you make a mistake
- ★ to be able to talk and have people listen
- ★ to be able to work alone and with others
- ★ to get help when we need it
- ★ to be able to choose what we read and write.

Over the next few days I set aside time to explore this question. First, we sorted the slips of paper into piles and then we named each pile: *materials*, *safety*, *talk*, *choice*, *time*, and *play*. Small groups of students rotated among the piles, leaving questions or comments. Reading through these, I was struck by how these children perfectly exemplified the complexities of interpreting rights from varied perspectives. Questions included:

- ★ If some people have a right to talk and others have a right to a quiet place to work, who gets to have their right?
- ★ What if not everyone needs the same amount of time for something?
- ★ How much choice are we really talking about?

For our next conversation I charted some of their thoughts and asked, "How is it possible for us to have these rights, especially if they don't look the same for everyone?"

Fahmida spoke first. "Maybe some people get them sometimes and other people get them other times, and we just have to remember that we all get ours sometimes?"

"Some *could* happen at the same time," Daniel offered, "like that half of the room is quiet and this half can talk."

Marya added, "Not loud talking though, or it won't be quiet over there."

"Yeah, so people still have to control themselves," warned Jaela.

Eli seemed to have something on his mind. "I want to say something about choice. I mean, can someone just choose not to do anything?"

Eric answered quickly, "Yeah, but we still get report cards."

I wondered, "Are you saying you should be able to choose not to do any schoolwork, but that there will be a consequence?"

Ivan was not having it. "No, choice doesn't mean just anything. You have to choose *right*. I don't think we should be able to choose just not to do work."

Eric replied thoughtfully, "Then that's not *really* a choice."

Rosie countered, "There are things we just have to do. We can still have choices without having every single choice."

"I think I'm hearing that we have rights, but we also have responsibilities," I mused.

"Yeah, like when Marya said about not talking too loud even on the talking side. If you're going to use that right, you still have to think about the quiet people."

"You know, adults have been grappling for as long as I can remember with what to do when some people's rights get in the way of other people's rights. Maybe they should've been asking fourth graders!"

After the conversation, I asked the class to collaborate in small groups, again rotating among our rights, to add responsibilities they thought were reasonable. The children had new clarity over what it really takes for a group of people to form agreements. This process took a few days longer than I had expected, thereby knocking my plans off-kilter. It was worth it. I felt such privilege in being among students who were active stewards of the learning that was happening in that room rather than just beneficiaries of it. In the end, our chart was very different than in years past.

It's worth noting that this process corresponds to civic participation practices in many states' social studies standards. On my part, I gained an important skill enabling me to spend less time on management and more on teaching.

Rights of Learners

Time We don't work at the same pace and we don't have to spend the same amount of time as everyone.

Choice We choose our own topics, how and when we'll work, how we'll focus our studies.

Talk We can learn from each other. We talk through ideas before writing them down. We get to disagree and change our minds.

Safety It's ok to take a risk. We treat each other well with our bodies and words.

Play We can learn about things by exploring, experimenting, and playing.

Chart of rights and responsibilities as learners

NEW YORK STATE SOCIAL STUDIES FRAMEWORK CIVIC PARTICIPATION PRACTICES

- Demonstrate respect for the rights of others in discussions and classroom debates, regardless of whether one agrees with the other viewpoints.
- Participate in activities that focus on a classroom, school, or community issue or problem.
- Identify the role of the individual in opportunities for social and political participation in the class, school, or local community. Show respect in issues involving difference and conflict; participate in negotiating and compromising in the resolution of differences and conflict.
- Identify situations in which social actions are required.
- Identify social and political responsibilities at the classroom, school, and community levels.

© 2017 NYSED. Used with permission.

What Is Collaboration Play?

This category of playful exploration has been part of my teaching practice longer than any of the others in this book. On my way to describing *what* Collaboration Play is, I need to take a little detour through *why* it's important. Learning is a largely social act and classrooms are social environments. Feelings of fear, anxiety, and competition—feelings that loom large for tweens—stand in the way of learning. Collaboration Play lays the groundwork for having a playful mindset *all the time*, even when we're not explicitly engaged in play. The experiences in this chapter support a classroom culture of safety to take risks, learning from mistakes, and seeking and offering help—*We're in this together.*

Collaboration Play also has important implications in the conversation about equity and access. The myth of the lone creative genius is exactly that: a myth. An overwhelmingly white and male one. Classrooms that favor individual achievement over collective accomplishments tend also to favor those most fluent in the ways of our dominant culture. The message for everyone else is, "Greatness isn't for you," or possibly, "If you learn to talk, dress, and act like us, you could be great," but definitely not, "There's a place for all of us at this table."

Clapp (2017) describes an antidote to the "lone genius" myth in classrooms that immerse students in "participatory creativity." The success of collaborative endeavors, he says, rests on understandings that directly contradict the traditional American paradigm of genius. The first is that people are not inherently creative or uncreative; *ideas* are creative. The second is that "creativity is not an individual capacity, but rather a socially distributed and participatory process" (1).

The explorations in this chapter support classroom structures, habits, and mindsets that include all students in having and developing ideas. I call this "collaboration play" rather than "collaborative play" because all of the play in this book is collaborative. In this chapter, *collaboration itself* becomes the material being played with. Students playfully explore processes, such as group conversations, problem-solving, and time management, that they will need to use well in their academic learning. As they reflect on the successes and challenges of the explorations, they become more skillful and self-directed learners.

Consider It

The ability to collaborate in school (and in the workplace) relies on two important understandings, of self and of the group. Learners must discover their own capabilities and acknowledge, without shame or competition, the strengths of others. I frame this understanding not as "We all have strengths and weaknesses" but as "We all have strengths. Sometimes they overlap and sometimes they don't. It's important to have a range of strengths in a group." In this way, children come to see the strengths of others as a benefit rather than as a personal shortcoming. Collaboration Play enhances learning in three main ways:

- ★ in support of *becoming a learning community*
- ★ as a way to *develop the skills of collaborative discourse*
- ★ to *increase investment in and ownership of learning*.

Become a Learning Community

We all want our classrooms to feel like communities of invested learners who feel safe taking risks. This can be difficult as students approach adolescence; they've become hyperaware of how others perceive them, but not yet fully aware of how their words and actions affect others. Or, more simply, it can be mortifying to make a mistake publicly but perfectly natural to point out a classmate's mistake. During these years, children also develop a keen ability to discern adult authenticity. Words like *respect* and *kindness* too often become the hollow school-speak children use around adults to either be or appear compliant. We must truly invite children into the conversation about expectations if we expect them to honor them.

These explorations involve asking students to consider the various human beings in the room, along with their quirks, foibles, strengths, interests, challenges, habits, preferences, and traits. It's not about everyone being friends. It's about being mutually invested in everyone's learning. We're not competing against one another—we're not even competing against other classes—we're competing, if at all, to continually outgrow *ourselves*. We do this by situating conversations about respect and kindness within specific experiences and by allowing students to experience firsthand the ways that these traits help them meet their own stated goals.

Develop the Skills of Collaborative Discourse

Children naturally use talk as a tool for developing ideas and, in play, learn conventions of collaborative discourse from one another. They don't need an adult to set a purpose or topic or to press them to support their thinking. Without raising hands, they figure out when to speak and when to listen. Peer feedback teaches them how to disagree or present alternatives, and when finding consensus or compromise better serves the shared goal of keeping the play going. The fact that these skills don't often transfer into the classroom doesn't mean that children don't have them. It just means they don't yet know how to apply them in a completely different setting.

The explorations in this chapter aim both to enable children to use the skills they have and to teach explicitly new skills they'll need in academic discourse. This happens first by bringing students into the shared purpose instead of setting it from the top down. Opportunities to grapple with ideas and topics students have chosen are essential to their conversational abilities. As they internalize the habits of collaborative discourse, teachers can then shift the content to academic topics.

Take Ownership of Learning

Investment in learning must be accompanied by students' deepening understanding of themselves as individual learners within the collaborative community. As a person who grew up with attention deficit hyperactivity disorder (ADHD), I learned early to perceive my weaknesses and inabilities. I worked harder to try to have other people's strengths. This was exhausting and did little for my confidence. It wasn't until much later that I was able to focus my efforts on recognizing and maximizing my strengths rather than hiding and minimizing my weaknesses. Identifying, without judgment, the strengths they do and don't have enables students to focus on their learning with more enjoyment and less anxiety.

Increased joy and decreased anxiety are prerequisites for taking ownership of learning. Next is the knowledge that one matters—that one is heard and acknowledged—as a key player in one's own educational process. We must communicate, not just with words but with our actions in the classroom, that we have high expectations of our students, that we trust their intentions, that we see approximation for what it is, and not the failure it might feel like. The explorations in this chapter, as different as they are, empower students to drive their own learning.

Imagine It

Let's look now at some examples of how collaboration can become the subject of playful exploration. Notice how these explorations have value in their own right but also have the power to lift student engagement in more traditionally academic pursuits.

Ideal Learning Environment

The last people ever consulted on decisions about school design, curriculum, or structuring a school day are the students who will be experiencing the effects of these decisions. In this exploration, students work first individually and then in small groups to imagine, discuss, and represent their vision of an ideal learning environment. By starting a school year with an invitation to collaboratively envision an environment in which they will be able to do their best learning, you communicate to students that their needs and ideas matter to you. Collaborative conversations require students to think about themselves as learners and articulate what does and doesn't work for them at school. Finally, the act of considering everyone's ideas and the available resources becomes an early problem-solving activity that builds a sense of community.

The suggestion that adults don't often ask students for input, but you want to do just that, is a pretty surefire way to spark student interest in this exploration. Invite students to consider and write a little about questions such as these:

- ★ What makes learning feel good?
- ★ What makes learning feel bad?
- ★ What do you hope your journey through this year looks like?
- ★ What do adults need to understand about how you learn?
- ★ What do adults need to understand about school socially?
- ★ What would a school day look like if it was perfect for you as a learner?

Write a few of these questions on a chart and ask students to choose the one(s) to which they feel connections. Invite them to respond, first individually. They can draw, write, make comics, or use bullet points; it should feel like an opportunity for expression rather than an assignment.

After students have had some time to reflect individually, form small groups of students who will share their individual ideas and then work together to create a representation (anywhere on the spectrum between literal and metaphorical) of their ideal learning environment. Give them materials to plan and sketch their visions. These could be any size, but probably not smaller than a piece of twelve-by-eighteen-inch drawing paper. Throughout this process, you might encourage groups to pause and walk around the room, looking at what other groups are doing. At the end of each period of work, have a brief share-out for groups to say a little about their work.

When all the representations are finished, hang them up and host a gallery walk, in which students circulate silently and look at all the pieces. In the final reflection discussion, pay attention to recurring ideas to compile a short

A fourth grader sees her path through the school year as a river.

One group's poster depicting ideals for their learning community

list of qualities the class can agree to maintain in support of everyone's best learning.

Soft Start

I first heard about Soft Starts at a workshop given by Harvey "Smokey" Daniels and later read about it in his book, *The Curious Classroom* (2017). After borrowing my copy, a fifth-grade teacher came to me excitedly asking if she could implement a Soft Start. I was only too happy to support her in anything that would enable students to transition more easily into school and acknowledge their human needs. What happened next was a pattern I've seen over and over as a teacher: a small investment of time raised the quality of the rest of the school day for her and her students.

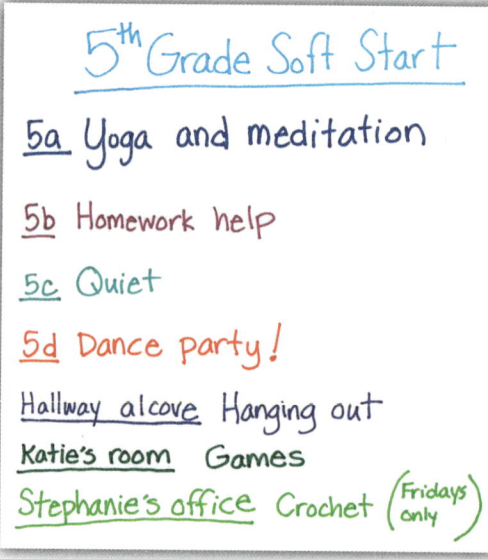

Chart of Soft Start options and locations

After having Soft Starts in place for a few weeks, teachers reported fewer interruptions and distractions and greater focus throughout the school day. Students reported less stress and greater enjoyment of their days in school. Win-win, as far as I can tell.

The transition from home to school requires a complete shift in focus and mental state. Sometimes it means getting ready to work, despite having strong emotions or thoughts about things happening outside of school. Many students' important social interactions happen at school. When we expect them to come into the classroom and immediately be ready for the day ahead, we go against their instincts to connect and check in. Soft Starts give students a buffer zone between not-school and school. They come to recognize where they are and where they need to be to start a day of learning. They can then learn to determine what they need on any given day to make this transition, whether it's quiet reflection, boisterous movement, conversation, or something else.

To facilitate this, my colleague explained the concept of a Soft Start to her class, asking what would help students feel ready to start the school day. Based on their responses, she set up areas of her room and a nook in the hallway outside. On arrival, students were able to socialize, read or write quietly, practice dance moves, get help with homework, or play games for fifteen to twenty minutes. Creating that many spaces was challenging but doable in her smallish classroom; however, when the other fifth-grade teachers caught wind of it (of course their students wanted the same thing), the team was able to pool their resources. Now teachers could designate their rooms for quieter or louder activities and students could choose where to softly start their days.

Strategic Mini-Unit

In these brief explorations, students work in pairs or triads to play a game or solve a puzzle, but the goal is to study and document their collaborative strategies and approaches. Games and puzzles that are simple to learn and don't require many sophisticated materials—tic-tac-toe, Nim or Nim Jr., Babylon, and Lines and Dots, for example—work well for this kind of exploration. Teach students the rules for the game if they aren't already familiar with them, then invite them to work in pairs to figure out if there are any strategies to increase the odds of winning the game. They'll need to record their play on paper, eventually creating a poster detailing their findings.

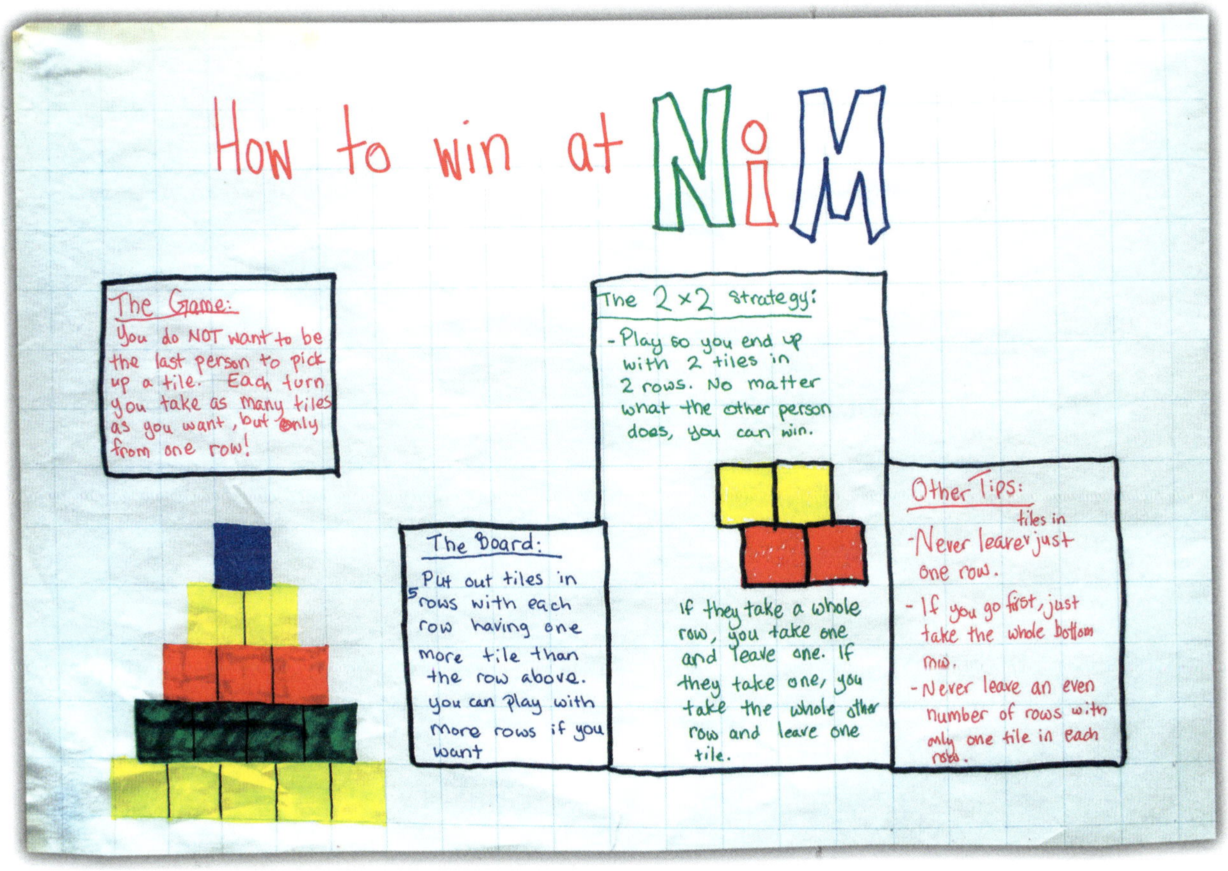

Students have figured out how to win at Nim.

Play Attention!

Pentominoes and The Seven Bridges of Königsberg are puzzles that work well. Introduce the puzzle and invite students to work in pairs or triads to solve it, documenting their solutions (or efforts toward a solution) on a poster or chart.

Any of these explorations works nicely in the beginning of a school year and can be framed as an early math unit that focuses on thinking systematically, noticing patterns, and clearly communicating thought processes—important practices for mathematical learning. Playing games and solving puzzles can also bring a shot of energy to the dark days of January or the long month of March. A study of collaborative strategy can take anywhere from a few days (if you focus on only one game or puzzle) to a couple of weeks (if you move from a simpler game to a more complex one).

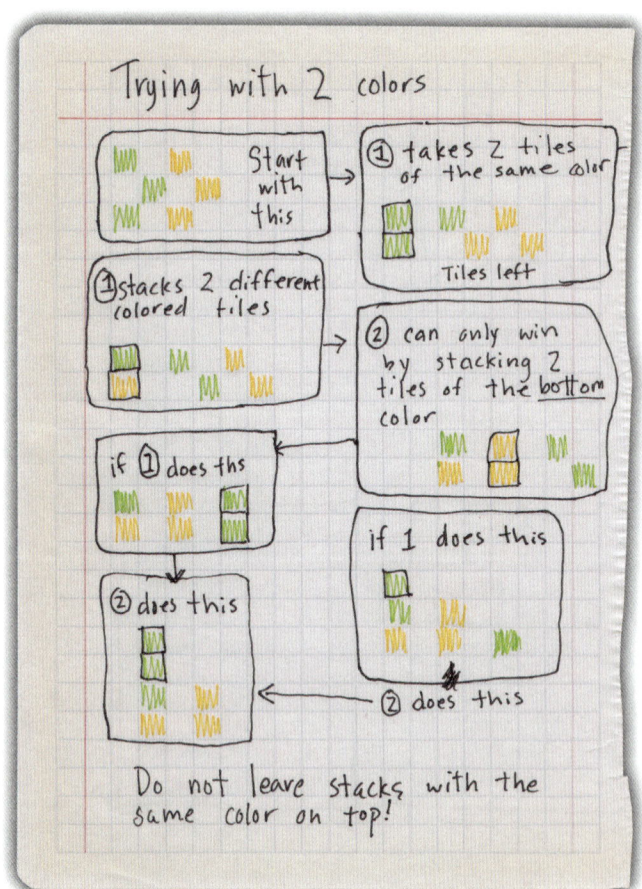
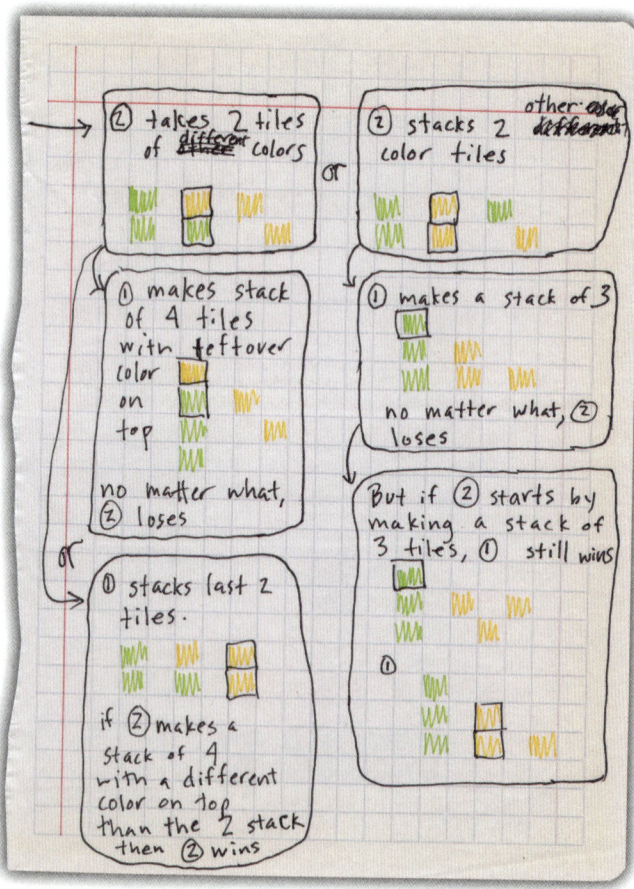

Partners try playing Babylon with only two colors as they look for winning strategies.

The reflection after this kind of play should focus on the collaboration as well as the ideas of thinking systematically, noticing patterns, and clearly communicating thought processes.

- ★ How do you know you (got them all, completed the puzzle, figured it out . . .)?
- ★ How did you work through the puzzle or process?
- ★ Do you both/all agree?
- ★ How did you figure out how to explain it to others?

Circle of Talkingness

Yes! *Talking about ideas* is a thing to be played with! Students can play with whole-class discourse the same way they play with plastic polygons—to learn what works and what doesn't and to become more skillful in using talk as a tool. These circles are periodic whole-class conversations directed by students, with little adult input. They can be messy, but over time students themselves decide on norms (with teacher support). Group discourse is challenging, and even adult models of large-group conversation usually include a moderator. When we give children the opportunity to participate in this kind of conversation, they practice:

- ★ listening to one another and not just the teacher
- ★ following a thread
- ★ tabling a thought if its moment passes
- ★ intuiting when to speak and when to yield
- ★ being aware of airtime
- ★ putting complicated ideas into words others can understand.

I have also called these Campfire Talks and, simply, class discussions. The term Circle of Talkingness came about when a class wanted to vote on what to call these discussions. A few students made suggestions and this one won. I was relieved that Oral Oval wasn't the top pick.

Learning to talk without the teacher is excellent preparation for more formal models of discourse, such as Socratic Circles or debate, and the practice also supports almost all the New York State Next Generation English Language Arts standards for speaking and listening.

Students often ask big questions or make bold statements, which we can't always pursue in the moment. If you jot these down, or ask students to, when they arise, you'll have the fodder you need for implementing student-led conversations. Introducing these conversations early in the year will support community building, though they can be launched anytime. Set aside a full period for the first discussion, so you can "press the pause button" and reflect

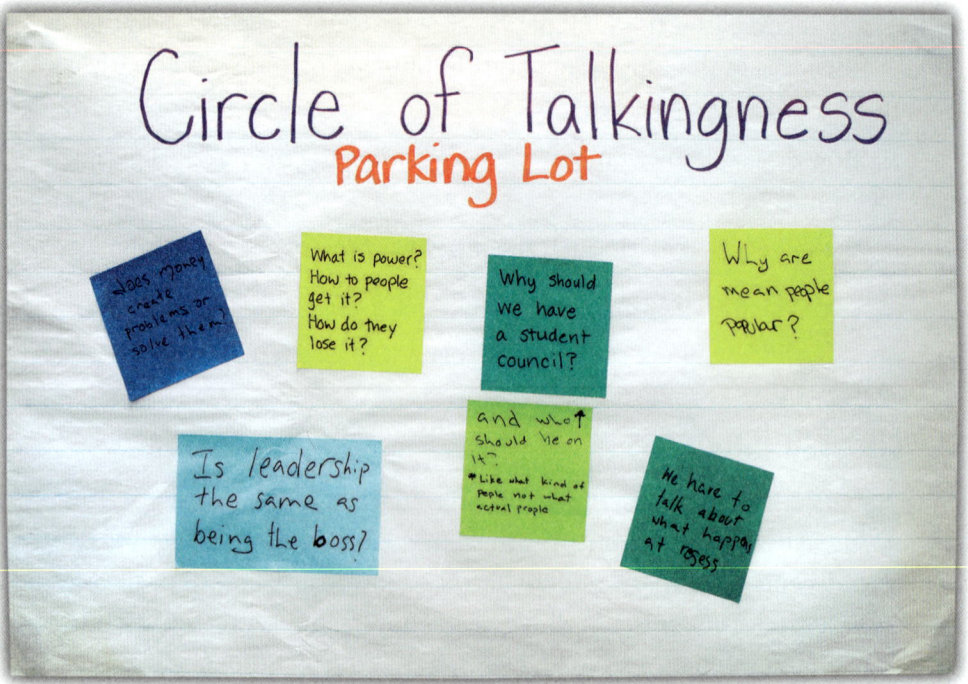

Parking lot for suggested topics

with students a few times. Keep the first few tries no more than a week apart as you co-construct norms with the class. After that, how often you engage in the conversations is up to you and your class.

If students are to outgrow traditional (teacher-directed) forms of classroom discourse, they must have opportunities to approximate. This will require a tolerance for messy conversations, opportunities to reflect together about how to improve them, and more practice. Most classroom discussions I observe follow a pattern of question-answer-feedback, with little opportunity for students to speak directly to one another or to initiate their own questions.

It's not that teachers *want* to control student talk; it's just that when students aren't leading the discourse or posing ideas, we often step in and do it for them. And we keep waiting for them to learn how to do it. Well, they're not going to if we don't invest some time and effort in teaching them how. This means giving students time and freedom to approximate and reflect, which is messy. Really messy.

These playful explorations are designed to allow students to approximate—really get into the weeds—with group discourse, reflect on the experience, and coauthor norms. In Addressing Challenges with Circle of Talkingness (p. 113), I've included a few simple moves you can use to address some common challenges.

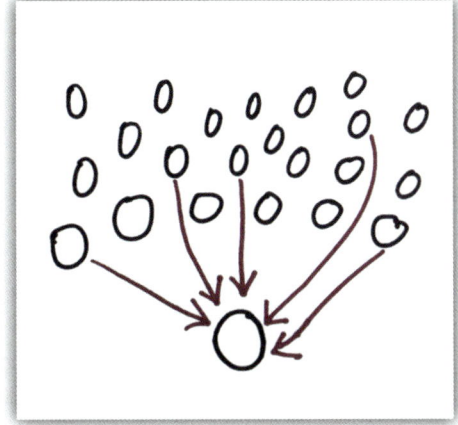

Traditional classroom talk patterns are controlled by the teacher.

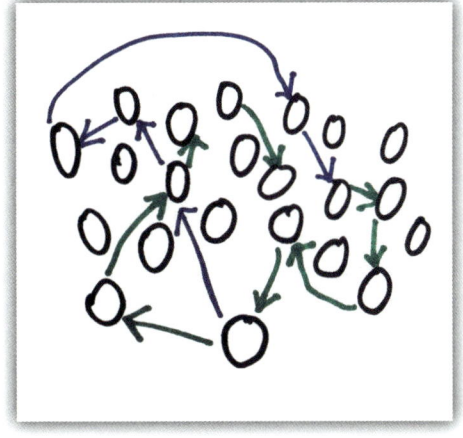

As they gain confidence, more students contribute and the teacher becomes more of a facilitator than a director.

ADDRESSING CHALLENGES WITH CIRCLE OF TALKINGNESS	
POSSIBLE CHALLENGE	WHAT MIGHT HELP?
Crickets—nobody talks	Ask the person whose topic it is to start. Remind students that in this kind of conversation, the teacher isn't deciding who speaks and when.
Everyone talks at the same time	Let it go for a bit to see if students themselves address the issue. Call a time-out to process the problem. Use a system for each speaker to call on the next speaker (for example, show a thumb if you have something to say and the speaker will choose a thumb).
Random topic changes	Let it go for a bit to see if students themselves address the issue.
The same few people say a lot and the same other few remain silent	Call a time-out and ask what students notice about whose voice has been heard or not heard. Introduce the concept of "airtime." (This may lead to the question of responsibility in group conversations, to be tabled for another time.) Introduce the convention of saying something like, "I'm curious about what you think, X."

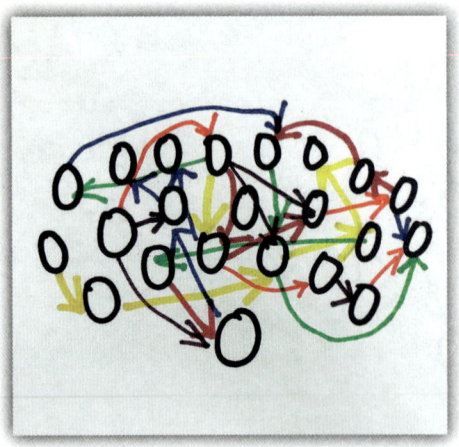

While the teacher might still be part of the conversation, many exchanges happen between and among students, without teacher input.

With continued practice and reflection, students develop the capacity to collaborate in talk and, suddenly one day, you find yourself proudly listening in on a powerful conversation that is happening without you!

Learning Plan

The Learning Plan, an idea I got from Ann Marie Corgill, is an opportunity for students to choose what they will work on and for how long, occurring when you have a stretch of time in the classroom with no specials. This exploration is designed to support students' awareness of how time seems to pass depending on what they're doing, how long things tend to take, and how to manage time when they have a choice, eventually empowering them to take control of their work processes. For example, as a writer, some days I can sit and work on a piece for hours, and I resent my schedule for pulling me away. Sometimes I *need* to be away from a draft, reading or researching, or just playing around in my notebook. Students feel the same way!

Invite students to make a Learning Plan by giving them each a sheet with a table of ten-minute increments and a list of things they must and may work on—reading notebook entries, working on drafts, independent reading, a math investigation, word work, and so on. The students' job is to think about how much time they want to spend on each thing, filling the block of time. Individual students can put in what they want, in any order they want. Try not to front-load too much advice (you want *students* recognizing problems and coming up with solutions), but do point out that anything they want to work on with other students will mean coordinating schedules.

To achieve this, there will be a lot of, shall we say, approximation. The first day will be a mess. But out of this mess emerges a lot of reflection,

This learning plan is an early approximation. The student thought he could get a lot done in ten minutes but didn't account for time to transition between activities.

and a major investment from the students in making it work so that they can do it again. With time, they will create more realistic and responsible plans.

The choice inherent in Learning Plans adds a playful dimension to everything students do, and with a little experience, they can come up with guidelines for making their plans and you'll be able to schedule them on a regular basis. Although the primary purpose is to empower students to manage their time and effort, the Learning Plan also helps you take charge of your teaching. Because you are no longer boxed into a set schedule, you can work with students individually or in small groups with more frequency and flexibility, which leads to more purposeful differentiation and better conferring.

How did this Learning Plan work for you today?
Not so great. I did not leave time to put away things I used and get the next stuff I needed.

A reflection page is on the back of every Learning Plan.

What did I learn today?

After each block of time, write a brief reflection about what you did. It could include:
- What you learned or discovered
- What you're proud of ✓
- What was hard ✓ ✓
- How someone helped you
- What you'd like to share ✓
- What you need to do next
- Anything else you think is important ✓

Polygon/ Angle Work — *I was hard because the group had a disagreement.*

Word Work — *I'm proud that Isa and I distinguished 'corps' and 'corpse'.*

Test Essay — *It was hard because I realized that two of my details were pretty much the same, and had to change them.*

Read Aloud — *Memoirshare I think it was important that we got to listen to other memoirs.*

What else did you do? *Independant Reading*

Name: Leelah
An important goal for today is *have time to read*

Time	Learning Focus
8:30-9:00	Arrival, Morning Meeting, Make Learning Plan
9:05-10:00	Finish Poster (9:05), Gallery Walk (9:25), Share (9:40)
10:00-11:00 (60 minutes)	W.W.M. 10:00-10:15 (15), W.C.E. 10:18-10:47 (20), 10:45- Test Group meet Stephanie, I.R. 10:47-10:00 (13)
11:05-11:50	Read Aloud Memoirs, Go over Test Essay
11:50-12:10	Read Aloud
12:15-1:15	Recess and Lunch
1:15-2:00	Gym
2:05-2:15	Pack Up and Clean Up
2:15	Teach & Share: Jillian

Options:
- Word Work Menu (15)
- Write Chickadee Essay with Checklist (20)
- Pocket Work
- Independent Reading
- Independent Writing
- Class Blog
- Kidblog

I need help with _____
I can help others with _____

A couple of weeks of practice leads to a more realistic Learning Plan.

Plan It

Lots of Collaboration Play requires you to tolerate messiness and remain patient through approximation, so begin your planning process with an honest self-assessment of how much of that you can handle at once. Although some of these explorations fit naturally into the launch of a new school year (envisioning the ideal learning environment, for example), others can wait. The Circle of Talkingness, for example, can be introduced in September or March. I guess my point is *Know thyself*. After you have some experience letting students play with collaboration, you'll have a much better understanding of how the timing should work for your specific situation.

Students are used to activities and time frames being decided by adults and usually don't know how those decisions are made. You will have to start small, with some low-risk exploration and reflection, if it is going to work. Don't give up after just one or two rough tries!

The Framework in Action for Collaboration Play

INVITE

Invitations for these explorations should spark interest in the dual purposes of academic learning and social-emotional well-being. The play you're inviting students to engage in should help them develop a personal investment and accountability for their own learning, while also being aware and respectful of others.

★ *People make decisions about how school should go without ever asking children. What would you like these people to know?*

★ *The other day Sam made a really interesting comment and I want you all to be able to discuss it together, without me having to direct the conversation. What do you think that would take?*

★ *In school we tend to do everything together, at the same time, for the same amount of time. I'm not sure if that always matches what everyone needs. I wonder if there are some days when whatever we're doing feels too long or not long enough. I have an idea that would give us some choice about how much time we spend on different kinds of work.*

(continues)

The Framework in Action for Collaboration Play *(continued)*

PLAY

Observe

As students playfully collaborate, observe how they interact with one another and how they approach the problem. Try to observe without correcting or redirecting. Instead, let curiosity guide you.

- ★ Are students competing or collaborating?
- ★ Do they appear to listen to one another? Is anyone either unwilling to accept other ideas or too willing to let go of their own?
- ★ Are students trying things haphazardly or following a systematic approach?
- ★ Are they discussing their plans or working separately?
- ★ Does group/partner work or talk reflect the input of everyone involved?
- ★ Do you see an evolution of thinking?

Provide Lean Input

Offer questions or thoughts that encourage self-reflection or help students find words to articulate complicated ideas. As they explore, ask questions such as:

- ★ *Has everyone's voice been heard?*
- ★ *How are you dealing with disagreements? Is it working? Are there other ideas?*
- ★ *How can you show/explain this idea/process?*
- ★ *What do you need in this situation?*
- ★ *What would be helpful to do if this happens again?*
- ★ *Do you need to make a change?*
- ★ *How would you like mistakes to be handled—yours and other people's?*

Keep an eye out for students who have difficulty articulating their needs. This is frustrating! Sometimes a break from the classroom is all a student needs. Sometimes concrete suggestions are more helpful.

- ★ *You can say that you need a few more minutes to think about it. Or you and your group could agree on a hand signal if you prefer.*
- ★ *Try telling your group that you feel like your idea was ignored. They might not know.*

(continues)

The Framework in Action for Collaboration Play *(continued)*

REFLECT

Reflection is a way to solidify learning about content and community, so make sure to address both. Whether you reflect purely in conversation or also in writing, some possible questions to include are:

★ *When you collaborate, what works well?*

★ *What do you appreciate in others?*

★ *What have you realized about yourself and others?*

★ *What do you need to thrive in this community?*

When things don't go so well, consider class problem-solving meetings as a structure to ensure voices are heard and to solicit suggestions from the class.

★ References ★

Almon, Joan. 2013. *Adventure: The Value of Risk in Children's Play*. College Park, MD: Alliance for Childhood.

Bergen, Doris. 2009. "Play as the Learning Medium for Future Scientists, Mathematicians, and Engineers." *American Journal of Play* 1 (4): 413–28.

Bruner, Jerome S., Alison Jolly, and Kathy Sylva. 1976. *Play—Its Role in Development and Evolution*. New York: Basic Books.

Clapp, Edward P. 2017. *Participatory Creativity: Introducing Access and Equity to the Creative Classroom*. New York: Routledge, Taylor & Francis Group.

Daniels, Harvey. 2017. *The Curious Classroom: 10 Structures for Teaching with Student-Directed Inquiry*. Portsmouth, NH: Heinemann.

Dansky, Jeffrey L. 1980. "Make-Believe: A Mediator of the Relationship Between Play and Associative Fluency." *Child Development* 51 (2): 576. doi:10.2307/1129296.

Dansky, Jeffrey L., and Irwin W. Silverman. 1973. "Effects of Play on Associative Fluency in Preschool-Aged Children." *Developmental Psychology* 9 (1): 38–43. doi:10.1037/h0035076.

De Koven, Bernard Louis. 2016. "We Study Play Because Life Is Crap." *A Playful Path* (blog), March 27. https://www.aplayfulpath.com/we-study-play-because-life-is-crap/.

Delpit, Lisa. 2006. *Other People's Children: Cultural Conflict in the Classroom*. New York: New Press.

Duncker, Karl. 1945. "On Problem-Solving." *Psychological Monographs* 58 (5): i-113. doi:10.1037/h0093599.

Dweck, Carol S. 2016. *Mindset: The New Psychology of Success*. New York: Ballantine Books.

Eichsteller, Gabriel, and Sylvia Holthoff. 2009. "Towards a Pedagogic Conceptualisation of Risk." *The Therapeutic Care Journal*. September 1. https://www.thetcj.org/in-residence/towards-a-pedagogic-conceptualisation-of-risk.

Elkind, David. 1967. "Egocentrism in Adolescence." *Child Development* 38 (4): 1025. doi:10.2307/1127100.

———. 1985. "Egocentrism Redux." *Developmental Review* 5 (3): 218–26. doi:10.1016/0273-2297(85)90010-3.

Ferry, Beth, and Tom Lichtenheld. 2015. *Stick and Stone*. New York: HMH Books for Young Readers.

Garvey, Catherine. 1990. *Play*. Cambridge, MA: Harvard University Press.

Gray, Peter. 2008a. "The Value of Play II: How Play Promotes Reasoning." *Psychology Today*. December 4. https://www.psychologytoday.com/us/blog/freedom-learn/200812/the-value-play-ii-how-play-promotes-reasoning.

———. 2008b. "Value of Play III: How Children Confront Life's Challenges." *Psychology Today*. December 16. https://www.psychologytoday.com/us/blog/freedom-learn/200812/value-play-iii-how-children-confront-lifes-challenges.

———. 2009. "Play as a Foundation for Hunter-Gatherer Social Existence." *American Journal of Play* 1 (4): 476–522.

———. 2011. "The Decline of Play and the Rise of Psychopathology in Children and Adolescents." *American Journal of Play* 3 (4): 443–63.

———. 2015. *Free to Learn: Why Unleashing the Instinct to Play Will Make Our Children Happier, More Self-Reliant, and Better Students for Life*. New York: Basic Books.

Groos, Karl. 1898. *The Play of Animals*. Translated by Elizabeth L. Baldwin. New York: D. Appleton and Company.

———. 1901. *The Play of Man*. Translated by Elizabeth L. Baldwin. New York: D. Appleton and Company.

Gwynne, Fred. 1999, 1970. *The King Who Rained*. New York: Aladdin Paperbacks.

Hauck, William E., and John W. Thomas. 1972. "The Relationship of Humor to Intelligence, Creativity, and Intentional and Incidental Learning." *The Journal of Experimental Education* 40 (4): 52–55. doi:10.1080/00220973.1972.11011352.

Heard, Georgia. 1999. *Awakening the Heart: Exploring Poetry in Elementary and Middle School*. Portsmouth, NH: Heinemann.

Henricks, Thomas S. 2015a. *Play and the Human Condition*. Urbana, IL: University of Illinois Press.

———. 2015b. "Play as Experience." *American Journal of Play* 8 (1): 18–49.

———. 2016. "Reason and Rationalization: A Theory of Modern Play." *American Journal of Play* 8 (3): 287–324.

———. 2011. "Play as a Pathway of Behavior." *American Journal of Play* 4 (2): 225–53.

Isen, Alice M., Kimberly A. Daubman, and Gary P. Nowicki. 1987. "Positive Affect Facilitates Creative Problem Solving." *Journal of Personality and Social Psychology* 52 (6): 1122–31. doi:10.1037/0022-3514.52.6.1122.

King, Pete, and Justine Howard. 2016. "Free Choice or Adaptable Choice: Self-Determination Theory and Play." *American Journal of Play* 9 (1): 56–70.

LaFreniere, Peter. 2011. "Evolutionary Functions of Social Play: Life Histories, Sex Differences, and Emotional Regulation." *American Journal of Play* 3 (4): 464–88.

Lewis, Linda. 2000. "No Barricade to Success." *South Florida Sun-Sentinel*. March 6. https://www.sun-sentinel.com/news/fl-xpm-2000-03-06-0003031185-story.html.

Pellis, Sergio M., Vivien C. Pellis, and Brett T. Himmler. 2014. "How Play Makes for a More Adaptable Brain: A Comparative and Neural Perspective." *American Journal of Play* 7 (1): 73–98.

Ryan, Richard M., and Edward L. Deci. 2000. "Self-Determination Theory and the Facilitation of Intrinsic Motivation, Social Development, and Well-Being." *American Psychologist* 55 (1): 68–78. doi:10.1037//0003-066x.55.1.68.

Senninger, T. 2000. *Abenteuer leiten – in Abenteuern lernen*. Münster/Germany: Ökotopia

Shipley, D. 2013. *Empowering Children: Play-Based Curriculum for Lifelong Learning*. Toronto: Nelson Education.

Spolin, Viola. 2000. *Theater Games for the Classroom: A Teacher's Handbook*. Evanston, IL: Northwestern University Press.

Sutton-Smith, Brian. 1975. "Play: A General Facilitator of Associative Fluency." *Developmental Psychology* 11 (1): 104–. doi:10.1037/h0076108.

———. 2001. *The Ambiguity of Play*. Cambridge, MA: Harvard University Press.

Vygotsky, L. S. 1978. (first published 1933) *Play and Its Role in the Mental Development of the Child.* Trans. 1966 by Catherine Mulholland. From *Mind in Society: The Development of Higher Psychological Processes.* Edited by Michael Cole, Vera John-Steiner, Sylvia Scribner, and Ellen Souberman. Cambridge, MA: Harvard University Press.

Wagner, Tony, and Robert A. Compton. 2015. *Creating Innovators the Making of Young People Who Will Change the World.* New York: Scribner.

Watling, Sue. 2016. "Panic Buttons and Transitional States of Being." *Digital Academic: Negotiating Shifts in Digital Practice* (blog), February 26. https://digitalacademicblog.wordpress.com/tag/senningers-learning-zone-model/.

Wilson, Margaret Berry, and Lora M. Hodges. 2015. *Language of Learning: Teaching Students Core Thinking, Listening, and Speaking Skills.* Turner Falls, MA: Center for Responsive Schools, Inc.